The
HEALING POWER
of the
HUMAN VOICE

The
Healing Power
of the
Human Voice

Mantras, Chants, and Seed Sounds
for Health and Harmony

JAMES D'ANGELO

Healing Arts Press
Rochester, Vermont

Healing Arts Press
One Park Street
Rochester, Vermont 05767
www.InnerTraditions.com

Healing Arts Press is a division of Inner Traditions International

Library of Congress Cataloging-in-Publication Data
D'Angelo, James.
  [Healing with the voice]
  The healing power of the human voice : mantras, chants, and seed sounds for
health and harmony / James D'Angelo.
      p. cm.
  Earlier edition published in the U.K. under title: Healing with the voice: Thorsons,
2000.
  Includes bibliographical references and index.
  ISBN 1-59477-050-6 (pbk.)
  1. Music therapy. 2. Sound--Psychological aspects. I. Title.
  ML3920.D24 2005
  615.8'5154--dc22

                                                                    2005007694

Printed and bound in Canada by Transcontinental Printing

10 9 8 7 6 5 4 3 2 1

Text design and layout by Priscilla Baker
This book was typeset in Sabon, with Avenir and Minion as display typefaces

Dedicated to my great teachers
Nicolai Rabeneck
Dr. Francis C. Roles
Jan Gorbaty
Jean Catoire

Contents

Acknowledgments

I wish to express my gratitude to my wife, Georgina, who helped to edit the manuscript, taught me the inner workings of word processing, and without whose support the book could not have come to be. My thanks to my dear friend Brian Lee for his contributions to the Resources and support; to Serge Beddinghton-Behrens, Don Campbell, Jonathan Goldman, Grethe Hooper-Hansen, Solveig McIntosh, and Warren Kenton for being an inspiration in this endeavor; and to Rollin Rachele, Kay Gardner, and Linda Whitnall for contributing materials.

Preface

Music has always been central to my life. The performing of classical music and jazz, as well as my own improvisations at the piano, still remain acts of enchantment. There is a sense of wonder at what the combination of sounds which we call "music" can do to expand the emotions and heighten awareness. To make music from the printed notes on the page or from the imagination is to be transported to other worlds, experiencing moments of pure ecstasy. I had always wanted to know exactly what was happening to the listener of these sounds. What was actually going on at each level of the person bathed in the sounds I was producing?

In 1992 I was asked to lead a music workshop, something I had never done before. I observed how the participants let go of their personalities and became bundles of joy and liberation. They might as well have been nine-year-olds. Through a simplicity of means and fully-directed attention they allowed the sounds and rhythms they produced to be a method for tuning and thus purifying their human instrument—body, mind, and spirit. This first taste of working this way with music and sound encouraged me to draw together much diverse knowledge I had amassed about the esoteric aspects of music, which included the unique writings of one of my mentors, the French composer Jean Catoire. This went hand in hand with the practice of meditation and sacred dance, the experience of choral singing, the study of Indian music, and the investigation of the pioneers in the ever burgeoning field of sound therapy which had its beginnings in the late 1960s. All of these elements contributed to the evolution of my therapeutic sound workshops throughout the 1990s.

The result was a synthesis of knowledge and practice that I felt had a validity in helping others to safely reach the state of what can be termed *sound health*—a state in which the physical body feels totally relaxed, fine energy flows without inhibition, quietude of mind prevails and body, mind, and spirit are in unity. Just as musicians play their instruments I believed, and still do, that the coming into these states is the result of play, not work, because "to play" always suggests being at ease (free of dis-ease) and exuding joy. Such was this view that at first I called my sessions "playshops" not "workshops." However, possible participants must have thought that the sessions were for children and little response was received. And so, like everyone else, I had to call them "workshops" or "courses" and gave them the name Sound Body Sound Mind Sound Spirit with the subtitle Therapeutic Sound and Movement Workshops. Subsequently I have titled them Healing With The Voice, Healing Vibrations, and The Power of the Resonating Voice.

With each passing year, more and more practitioners using people's voices as the resonating instrument for sound therapy are appearing on the scene. Some teach a very specific tradition such as classical Indian music, Hindu or Buddhist Sanskrit chanting and overtone singing; others, like myself, are eclectic, drawing on both Western and Eastern sources. The directory of the Sound Healers Association produced in 1995 (see resources) has a listing of over 120 sound healers. There are many more now.

I hope that this book, which is the basis for all that I do in leading therapeutic sound workshops, will be useful to those who sense that their voices could be the instrument for healing themselves at any level and would like to make a start in this direction. You do not need to have had any previous experience using the voice in a therapeutic manner, not even singing, to make use of this book. Even I have no training as a singer. Equally, it can be a source book for musicians, particularly—but not necessarily—singers, who would like to conduct workshops of their own. Although I have not worked with people with any sort of physical or mental disability, it could be that some music therapists might find some of this material suitable for their patients in a clinical setting. Whatever the case, each person, being unique by definition, who decides to take up vocal sound as one of the many pathways to healing and wholeness, has to discover by experience what particular vibrations out of the many offer help to establish what they most desire—sound health in body, mind, and spirit.

JAMES D'ANGELO
GLOUCESTERSHIRE, ENGLAND
JANUARY 2005

An Introduction to Sound Healing

We live in a world that is alive with sounds, ever more so with the increasing prevalence of technology which has produced a relatively new environmental problem: noise pollution, from the bleeps of mobile phones to the roar of jet aircraft. Although people claim to desire peace and quiet, many are conditioned unconsciously to the numerous man-made sounds and noises and might actually find silence too much to bear. For the general public, noise pollution is not high on the list of the conditions that plague us. The desire not to have a silent world is typi-fied by all the background music people use when at work or even play, not to mention all the piped-in music in public places. It becomes a form of dependency for relaxation or simply a way of accomplishing two things at once.

It is no simple matter to dismiss the sounds of our environment and to try to exist in a world as silent as possible. First of all, we don't always have control of the situation. We can choose to turn off a radio but not to stop the sound of traffic on the high street. The sounds of our world each have their own quality and their absorption into our bodies, minds, and spirits will produce either positive or negative effects which are often not detected. And we are powerless to stop it, short of removing ourselves, because these patterns of vibration are physical and penetrate the whole of our being. We do not have to hear them to be affected: ears are not the only entry. For example, the abdominal region can experience the vibration of a pneumatic drill directly without hearing the ear-splitting noise that accompanies it.

When we do have choice, which sounds are beneficial? As human beings we are thoroughly a part of Nature—the mineral, plant, animal, and human kingdoms. Some mystics tell us that we have actually evolved through each of them; that within us is the knowledge of being a crystal, a flower, and a bird. Some scientists tell us that we are the very stuff of stars. Therefore we find ourselves in harmony with the sound of the oceans, rivers, streams, and waterfalls, the wind and its passage through trees, the rustling of leaves, the creaking of branches, rainfall, the songs of birds, dolphins and whales, the cries of certain animals and, at the human level, singing in all its forms, from the sweet sound of a solo folk singer to a 200-voice choir, as well as all sorts of musical ensembles whose instruments are constructed of natural substances. With these kinds of sounds we remember, either consciously or unconsciously, that we are universal beings on a journey to kingdoms of even higher frequencies. They are catalytic forces in our spiritual unfoldment that can carry us eventually beyond the current third dimension of our existence.

When we experience, in all these forms, the power of sound to transform our state, however briefly, and when there is a real sense of love, wonder and unity, it is natural to ask how we can consciously use the sound phenomenon to our benefit. Passively, it is in listening to music. Do you know anyone who does not listen to—or at least dance to—music? People are making all sorts of choices about the kind of music they listen to, often according to a particular mood they want to establish in themselves. Never before have we had such a wide spectrum of styles including the folk and classical music from many countries and all the music that is labeled "New Age." There are even further choices—to listen to live or recorded music and to acoustic or electronic instruments. Some limit themselves to one type of music or to only a few composers because these always seem to work their magic. This selection process is quite central to the work of the modern-day music therapist who has to correlate musical structure and hence mood with the needs of the patient. In some quarters this has become quite specialized* and there is even a school of music therapy specifically for the dying.† The how and why of making such choices is an arresting subject that is beyond the scope of this book. Suffice it to say that the passive approach of listening to organized patterns of vibration, which we call "music," is the predominant sound method used by people to change their state for the better, possibly entering a world of ecstasy and transcendence.

The passive approach of receiving vibrations into the body/mind/spirit complex as a form of sound therapy is nowadays not confined to listening to music. Particularly over the last twenty years a number of methods have been developed, all of which are based on the idea that human beings are a multitude of frequencies (rates of vibration) from the molecular level up to the bio-energetic field that surrounds the physical body. Unlike music, whose principal effect is on the emotions, these therapies are focused primarily on correcting frequency rates just as a tuner would do when adjusting the strings of a piano. These approaches, none of which have been accepted by the mainstream scientific establishment, take such forms as:‡

♪ Application of tones produced electronically or by crystals directly onto the body

♪ Sounding Tibetan singing bowls and gongs near to the body

♪ Absorbing the vibrations of multiple strings amplified by a specially designed table

---

* Guided Imagery and Music. See resources under this title.

† The work of Therese Schroeder-Sheker. See resources under "Music Thanatology."

‡ For further information, see resources.

♪ Receiving music physically by placing speakers near to and surrounding the body

Listening to:
♪ Tuning forks set in simple, pure ratios
♪ Music in which only the higher end of the sound spectrum is retained
♪ Particularly tuned sounds that are determined by analyzing the patterns of the voice
♪ Tones that have been calculated as corresponding to the chakras and even the bodies of the solar system

The active approach of actually making sound, especially with the voice, is chosen by far fewer people. Listening to the older languages in the world, particularly those of indigenous peoples, we hear how much they are like singing, suggesting that the natural state of the voice for communication was once singing, a far more varied form of vocal sound than our modern-day speech. So it is not a good sign of the times that there is a decline in many Western countries of singing within the educational systems. It may be taught to younger children but as the curriculum becomes quickly more demanding, singing is often put aside. It is not recognized that music of a certain quality has a very subtle way of building character and that group singing has some inherent moral and ethical effect on the participants. In referring to the effects of using the voice harmoniously, the composer Paul Hindemith quoted the German proverb that translates, "Bad men don't sing."[1] There is no doubt that choosing to sing with others on a regular basis will contribute to the maintenance of a good level of physical and mental health.

Speech aside, the human voice is brought into play automatically in expressing emotions. It performs a cathartic and cleansing function by laughing, crying, groaning, sighing, yawning, wailing and all sorts of natural sounds (see chapter 8). Ask yourself how often you laugh really heartily and you realize what opportunities are being missed for your well-being. These sounds are not consciously produced but, on the other hand, people all too often consciously suppress them because they may be considered childish or they have been taught to maintain some false sense of dignity by minimizing or even withholding such sounds. Yet, done with vigor, these sounds hold within them great power for healing.

We can take the process one step beyond natural sounds and singing and apply the voice consciously and therapeutically to our threefold nature of body, mind, and spirit. Singing is limited by its ever-changing character; it moves through many patterns of notes and words during its unfolding and is not meant to focus on any particular function. Therapeutically, it lacks a certain depth. However, if a choral group were to sing a certain phrase from J. S. Bach's *B Minor Mass* over and over again, who knows what effects it might have as it is given the time to do its work.

The conscious use of that musical instrument of musical instruments, the human voice, for the purpose of healing (however the word *healing* is interpreted—see chapter 3) revolves around four essential areas—the induction of natural sounds, toning, chanting, and overtoning. In all cases, soundwork is narrowly confined and repetitive so that it can be localized and allowed to be an ever-deepening process. This is not a new idea but one that has been revived in the West since the 1970s. For centuries the religious and philosophic traditions of the East have known the power of the voice as a healing instrument and a means of leading aspirants to higher states of consciousness. This knowledge has now become part of the repertoire of many practitioners in the sound therapy field and naturally forms an integral part of this book.

You are invited to go on a journey of discovery through the directed application of your voice. In many self-development courses, people are asked again and again to "let go" and to "allow." There is no better case for this than in allowing your voice its full freedom. This is not about the quality of your voice but the intent you place behind it. If you start from such preconceptions as, "I am tone deaf," "my notes are always off-key," "I don't have much breath," "my voice is generally weak," "I have only a few decent notes," or "my teachers told me I wasn't good at singing," then you will already be stopped in your tracks. There is no doubt that to do this soundwork you will need to be non-judgmental in the prejudicial sense. That is, only witness the results of the vibrations and do not keep harping on any limitations of your voice. Therapeutically, your vocal sounds can have as much potency as any trained voice, especially if you place a powerful desire behind them. And, of course, no one else will be listening to you even in a group setting, so there need be no anxiety of being judged.

From the many soundwork exercises and rituals presented in the succeeding chapters you will find some that resonate strongly with your nature and that you can practice on a regular basis. Each ritual is rich and concentrated and it does not take hours and hours of vocal soundwork to produce therapeutic effects. In conjunction with some form of meditative silence that inevitably follows the soundwork, natural sounds, toning, chanting, and overtoning are great forces leading you to become what you are meant to be: whole, the full integration of body, mind, and spirit.

2

The Nature of Sound and Vibration

"In the beginning was the Word and the Word was with God and the Word was God." This profound idea stated at the outset of St. John's Gospel in the New Testament is the very basis of humanity's existence. This concept is not confined to Western Christianity; it is reflected in the ancient cultures of India, China, Japan, Persia, Egypt, and Greece as well as among the North and Central American Indians whose cosmologies also tell how the universe came into being through the emission of an all-encompassing sacred sound. The very word *universe* can be defined as a "turning to the One" from *uni* = "one" and *verse* = "a turning." And *verse* also refers to poetry and music, so this stretches the meaning of universe to "one song," "one sounding," or even "one word." What is this *Word,* what sounded it, and what has become of it? First our imaginations have to conceive of a being, an initiator, or an ultimate Creator who exists in complete and utter stillness. This is difficult because everything in this world that has been studied by scientists, from sub-atomic particles to galaxies, is in movement. The Word in Latin is given as *Verbum*, equivalent to the English "verb," that which describes all kinds of action and movement. Creation is movement of one kind or another. It reverberates. For example, atoms are composed of particles of energy that are known to be in ceaseless motion, sometimes actually causing audible sound. Within the human sphere, meditators, especially the great Tibetan monks, can achieve high degrees of stillness and enter deeper realms of existence. Breathing, heartbeat, and brain waves slow down but nevertheless movement carries on within them. How could it be otherwise?

Before the beginning of time and space, the supreme Creator, existing in an absolute perfect equilibrium, desired to manifest a great play of forces which we witness as the universe and call "life." Into the limitless void it intoned and sent out an all-powerful seed vibration containing within it all possible forms or archetypes—invisible and visible, audible and inaudible. That is the Word, the vibration of vibrations, the sound of sounds, the tone of tones. In other words, it became *e-motional*, literally "moving out from." This primordial emotion, which is the vibration of love in its purest form, is a pulse or throb just as our hearts pulse or throb. It expanded into a wave-form generating an endless series of overtones and undertones, vibrations above and below the original tone operating at many levels of creation. These inaudible patterns of vibratory waves became the building blocks of creation and gave to matter its numberless forms, including us, and they continue to sustain it. The process works in reverse when a seed syllable is planted in the mind in the act of meditation. The seed is the form which transforms itself into a wave pattern and eventually dissolves into a pulse. To have a taste of how vibration shapes form, call to mind looking at the blades of a fan or propeller as they move faster and faster. Eventually they spin so rapidly that the eye begins to see a nearly solid circular object and not the separate blades. This is how we should see the world around us, and if we can we will understand that everything is one interconnected network of vibrational energies.

Vibration, or sound in its audible form, is the result of two opposing forces in the world. And without opposites and our desire to reconcile them, how could there be movement and therefore the energy of life itself? We should note that the word "energy" in Greek is *energia*, meaning simply "in movement." On the one hand there is a state of absolute stillness, seemingly non-existent in the universe; on the other, there is the Word which disturbed that utter repose. And in these forces we have the essence of vibration, the creative tension between the fluctuations of movement and emotion and their deep inclination to return to the state of absolute stillness. The very word *tone* from the Greek means "tension." Without this tension no sound could be produced from the human voice or any musical instrument.

The terms *sound* and *vibration* are essentially synonymous, as something must vibrate, that is move to and fro, in order for us to hear sound. However, it has to be accepted that this phenomenon occurs at many levels beyond the audible. Within the Vedic texts of Indian philosophy two kinds of sound are described—one that is *struck* and can be heard by our aural sense and one that is *unstruck,* the very fine vibrations of the Word beyond our ordinary hearing. Within the unstruck sound lies the world of archetypes, which some might call "the mind of God." This concept is embodied in the opening passages describing creation in the Book of Genesis. In particular, the Creator conceived a fundamental phenomenon in our world—Light. In order to manifest it, the Creator had to intone a sound, a fragment of the Word. "And God said, Let there be Light and there was Light." The very phenomenon of light is high frequencies of vibration far beyond audible sound. This concept was possibly understood by ancient people as evidenced by the researcher David Elkington's discovery that the derivation of the word "God" can be traced back to the word *Guth* in Old High Norse meaning literally "voice"[1] thereby connecting God to sound as well as light. Later in Genesis (2:19–20) there is a second instance of how vibration or sound creates forms. When the Lord God had shaped or conceived all the animals, beasts and birds, he lets Adam give each its name. Did these names or sound formulas give solidity to what were only archetypes? Do our own names given to us at birth in some way embody in sound who we are? As it is stated in Genesis, humanity was made in the image of God: we are a kind of microcosmic mirror that can reflect the one all-pervading consciousness. This suggests that we should emulate God and, by inference, Adam, and use our own voices to give birth to new and higher dimensions of ourselves as well as new forms to assist in establishing an environment conducive to such a rebirth.

The astrophysicists of our modern-day world have given credence to the existence of the Word. It has been described as the "Big Bang," an all-powerful spark that let loose floods of matter into the void of space where the process of the birth and death of stars continues. The sound of the original "bang" is still being detected in outer space, suggesting that the tone of tones goes on sustaining us and all creation. Emotionally and spiritually, it is better for us to identify with this original sound as the Word, the Great Resounding, or the Great Mantra. In Sanskrit the Word is given as the sound VAC, meaning "that which permeates the universe." This gives a profound, different meaning to the word *vacuum*. If an "a" is inserted as the motive force—vac(a)uum, a equation of unity is formed. VAC is equated with the supreme mantra AUM suggesting that what we name as a vacuum is actually an enormous energy field. Also, curiously, if the consonant L, the vibration of the root chakra in Tantra Yoga (see chapters 6 and 11), is inserted into the Word, we have the creation of the Wor(L)d.

From these concepts it is a small step to the visionary and age-old idea of the music of the spheres—that the vibrations of the planets in their orbits create a harmonious music perceived only by a few precious beings. The juxtaposition of these planetary vibrations forming musical ratios is the very basis of the astrological aspects—conjunctions, sextiles, squares, trines, and oppositions—which mark out features of a person's character. In this respect, the music of the spheres subconsciously echoes inside all beings.*

Thus, the Creator, the composer above all composers, desired to weave a universe of enchantment, a magical kingdom, and so he

---

* Relevant to this is the work of Michael C. Heleus which he calls Astrosonics. See resources under "Astrosonics."

chanted the Word from which would emerge a symphony of endless creation. To the great ancient cultures of the East, the Word's earthly realization is the sound of OM, or AUM in the Sanskrit version. The Greek alphabet represents the AUM as all embracing beginning with A(H)lpha and ending with OMega. It is further reflected in our being when put forward as I AM, in a unit of matter AtoM, in the first human AdaM, in spiritual assent AMen and, intriguingly, in the anagram of Amen, nAMe, our particular vibrational signature. This sound transferred itself to the language of Latin in the form of OMNES, the all-encompassing and all-pervasive. Therefore the Creator, by virtue of the Word, is OMnipotent and OMnipresent. The Hindus embody this concept in the expression "*Nada Brahma.*" These Sanskrit words translate as *Nada,* "sound," and *Brahma,* "both the Creator God and the universe," indicating that the Supreme Being, the cosmos and the phenomenon of sound are one and the same.

The very nature of tones, those individual pearls of sound, is that of the one and the many. Regularly vibrating objects, most especially the voice and musical instruments, are a conglomerate of frequencies. When any tone is sounded, innumerable higher sounds embedded in this fundamental arise out of it. These hidden sounds are called "overtones" or "harmonics." The various patterns of their presence and varying strengths determine the coloration of the sound. Two voices singing exactly the same frequency can be differentiated on the basis of their particular overtone structure which can be likened to the DNA or genetic blueprint of the sound. We hear any tone as wholeness, the one (the fundamental) and the many (the overtones) joined together. In like manner we can feel ourselves as one of the infinitude of overtones that emerge endlessly from the Word like the branches of a tree—worlds within worlds. This idea has a parallel in one of the current cosmologies in new physics that likens the universe to an enormous stringed instrument. The theory is that the fundamental particles of the cosmos are tiny snips of subatomic particle strings 100 billion times shorter than the diameter of the nucleus of an atom. The particle strings vibrate in predetermined ways and interact with one another to create the properties of the particles of matter.[2] From such a theory we can sense that the world is a vast chain of overtones of which we are a part, each person vibrating at his or her own particular frequency. This view offers a possible explanation of how all the universe is linked together. If we assume that linkage is instantaneous anywhere in the universe—the idea of omnipresence—then it must be densely packed with some special, as yet undetectable, carrier element. For one of the basic laws of the physics of sound is that the denser the transmitter the faster the vibrations will travel. This medium, unknown to science, could be what the ancients of India called *Akasha*, translated as the mysterious element "ether" but also as "sound." There is a subtle link between ether and that which is "eternal." It is the insertion of the letter H symbolizing the breath of God. According to the Vedic texts the element of ether was the first to appear out of the sounding of the Word. Subsequently the elements of air, fire, water, and earth emerged as the basic stuff of creation. On this basis every thought vibration has the capacity to affect the whole, and this view gives us pause to consider all the negative patterns of thought that are sent out continuously into this carrier field. It means that if sound can heal us, it also has the power to destroy when wrongly applied. Such an incident occurred when a French engineer, investigating the effect of sound on the human body, developed a large whistle that emitted sub-audio frequencies. When it was first tested by one of his technicians, the man's internal organs were ruptured and he died in an instant.[3]

How does this "sound" cosmological view of the world link to our physical, emotional, and spiritual well-being? First of all, connection is effected by the principle of resonance, from the Latin *re-sonare*, "to return to sound/vibration." The physics of sound contains two types of resonance—sympathetic and forced. Sympathetic resonance or vibration occurs when one vibrating object sets in motion another object which has an identical frequency. The well-known example of this is a singer shattering a glass due to over-resonating its exact sound frequency structure. Similarly there is the biblical story of Joshua and his army blowing trumpets and beating drums, encircling the walls of

Jericho and through an extraordinary resonance collapsing those walls. It is rather strange that scientists have used such an emotional word as "sympathy" to describe this phenomenon. Sympathy is another word for "love" and takes us back to the very first emotion—the Word.* Is it not like two people falling in love when their frequencies co-mingle and sympathetically resonate? Forced resonance takes place when the power of a vibrating object sets in motion another object no matter what the frequencies of the latter. For example, the vibrating strings on a violin or piano will resonate the wooden body of the instrument and, as a result, the sound will be amplified and resonate with a far greater intensity.

At the spiritual level we are all connected to the One Sound of Sounds but cut off from its full impact in varying degrees. The fact is that without the connection we cease to exist. Our conscious or even unconscious desire is to strengthen this connection substantially through the resonance that can be generated through our voices. When this is really tapped, its actual throb or pulse can be sensed, a release of fine energy can be felt and our emotions become free of negativity. This is our natural seed sound, what the Hindus call a mantra. Our emotions in turn are intertwined with our physical bodies through an energy field surrounding them, often called an aura. The cells, muscles, organs, glands, the blood circulation and nervous systems of the body and the auric field are all sound resonators and can be compared with a complex musical instrument. For that instrument to produce its most glorious sound, it has to be in perfect tune: every aspect of it vibrating at its correct frequency. This is the endpoint of holistic health where a person can feel totally and truly "at ease." On the other hand, when certain vibration patterns lose their correct frequencies and go "out of tune," then we become ill and acquire a "dis-ease."

---

* To quote physicist/inventor Dale Pond: "The common connecting link between substance and energy is vibration and common vibratory phenomena that connects vibration is 'sympathy.' In real human terms, we call sympathy or sympathetic vibrations LOVE. This is the Law that binds individuals together. This is the Law that binds molecules together." See recommended reading under General Interest.

It cannot be chance that the very word *sound* is used as an adjective to describe something that is well-ordered and without flaws. We speak of people being in "sound health" and of "sound mind" and of principles being "sound." The German word *Gesundheit* translates not only as "health" but also "soundness." The word *sound* is also used to describe certain bodies of water that are a channel between larger bodies of water. In German it is *sund*. The key words here are *water* as it relates to its movement in the form of waves and *channel*, for sound is a primary channel for reconnecting with the tone of tones—the Word. The letter "U" lies in the middle of the word *sound*. It is even found at the center of the supreme Eastern mantra AUM. Think of it as YOU, that you lie at the center of sound as a person—*per sonare*, a through-sound being.

Sound, as a therapeutic force in our lives, is not to be taken as just any audible vibration that enters our energy field and impacts on our nervous system. We are well aware that there are many sounds in our daily lives that disturb the balance of our health. Even inaudible vibrations in the form of ultrasound, for example, thought to be harmless, might have subtle adverse effects. Each of us has particular sounds that are upsetting or irritating, either physically or psychologically, because they are out of synchronization with our unique set of frequencies. For our well-being we should live, whenever possible, in a sound environment in tune with our nature and develop a discrimination about the forms of sound we absorb. When we develop a taste for the sounds, in whatever form, that lead us toward liberation and true happiness, then we will discover what many sound healers call "sacred sound"—that which is holy and gives us wholeness.

3

The Power of the Resonating Voice

The human voice is one of our greatest gifts. Linked to our mind, it presents an extraordinary mode of communication through speech, singing and all the natural sounds of our emotions. Yet how often is the voice used consciously to our benefit? So much time is spent in idle conversation where the voice is ruled by mercurial mind. The greater activity of the voice is singing, but how many of us engage in it? And as for the sounds of natural emotions, they are more often than not suppressed in us from an early age.

All of us have felt the power of human speech and know how it impinges on us even when it is not consciously directed. In it can be heard all manner of emotions and states of mind that can affect our own emotional and mental balance. For example, we often feel a great depletion of energy when we are abused verbally or are in the presence of someone pouring out inconsolable grief. Expressions such as anger, deep pleasure, humor, sorrow, fear, slyness, prodding, persuasiveness, and sympathy are effortlessly produced between the thought patterns of the mind and the voice. Even the meaning of a single statement such as, "It is necessary that I fulfill all my desires now" could be modified in many ways through the inflections and accents of speech. Subconsciously, we are all actors and we alter the sounds of our speech to our advantage. And often it is without intention. So imagine the greater power of the voice when it is consciously directed. Observe how political leaders project their voices to persuade the masses. One of the greatest examples of this was Hitler who incited and mesmerized the German people through his speeches.

The voice is one of the major keys to the character and state of a person. Without realizing it, we give away how we are feeling through the sorts of sound we produce. Relative states of relaxation and tension are reflected in our speech. Our essential nature is imprinted on all our utterances. We have all experienced voices that, no matter what emerges, grate on our nervous system while others seem soothing. On a worldwide scale, the character of a nation is mirrored by its language and the way it is spoken—the singing, open vowel sounds of Italian, the mellifluous, sensual tones of French, the clipped, closed-mouthed style of English, or the drawling sounds of the American South. Within these patterns come many variations, and individuals can be categorized by listening to the frequency level (high to low), speed, and volume of their voices. In order to detect these, the listening has to be done without becoming involved in the meaning of the words. Speech patterns also indicate that people fall primarily into different elemental types; that they are earthy, fiery, watery, or airy in character. The American polarity therapist John Beaulieu has developed a technique called Voice Energetics[1] for diagnosing health problems on the basis of the lack or excess of elemental patterns. Similarly, Hazrat Inayat Khan, founder of the Sufi Order in the West and master Indian musician, has written about the qualities and elemental characteristics of three basic types of voices.[2] One is indicative of power (*jelal*), another of beauty (*jemal*), and a third of wisdom (*kemal*). Within these categories can be found a mixture of elemental colorations with one usually predominating:

Earth: hope-giving, encouraging, tempting

Water: intoxicating, soothing, healing, uplifting

Fire: impressive, arousing, exciting, horrifying, awakening

Air: uplifting, calming, detached

Ether: inspiring, healing, harmonizing, convincing

Sometimes people will consciously change the sound of their natural voice in order to project an image of themselves. This unnatural sound may be assumed for professional reasons but, whatever the reason, the result could be a definite shift in the person's character. On the other hand, the mind is quite adept at modulating the voice as the situation demands. In fact, the study of acting, as it relates to the voice, would be beneficial in liberating our personality and tapping deeper levels of ourselves. Even taking into account such modulations, each person's vocal sound, like our fingerprints, is unique due to the particular patterns of the voice's overtones (see chapter 12). These patterns can be detected through the use of modern spectral analysis* and consequently the sounds of voices can even be used as a form of security identification.

Singing is the natural inclination of the voice and, therapeutically speaking, the next level beyond the act of speech. The language of early man, as it is with young children now, was sing-song in nature and perhaps closer to birdsong in inflection. We still hear this sort of sound today in African languages and those from the Far East. Their patterns of speech are far richer than those of English, cover a wider range of frequencies and contain a broader palette of overtones. Unquestionably it is healthy to sing because the voice box or larynx can create far greater resonance effects than it can in speaking, and unnatural speech patterns are often bypassed through creating singing sounds. Consider how in former times all sorts of workers accompanied their tasks with songs that so much eased their labors. And imagine the healing power

---

* For example, this is used as a diagnostic tool in the sound therapy known as Bioacoustics or Vibrational Retraining. See resources under "Selected Non-Vocal Therapies."

of such collectives, just as in a choir performing a choral work, where the vibrations are multiplied a hundredfold. In general, there has been a steady decline in all forms of community singing, particularly among the western European nations and the United States. When, if ever, did you last gather around a piano at a party and sing any sort of song? Too many people have become passive receptors of music instead of creating music themselves. Future generations will lose touch with a natural source of healing if they leave singing to entertainers who are not necessarily models for creating good vibrations.

Lying somewhere between speech and singing are the natural sounds of our emotions in such forms as laughing, crying, groaning, wailing, screaming, sighing, yawning, whistling, and humming. These sounds are our birthright and they are intended by nature to be purifiers, to release feelings, positive and negative. Remember that emotion means "a moving out from." Very common examples are a mother humming to her baby and a workman whistling. Children are a fount of natural sounds including many that just express joy and come out in the form of nonsense syllables. Perhaps they are not nonsense but fragments of some ancient-remembered language. But like so much else in childhood, they are put aside as we are molded into adults by our parents, teachers, and social environment. The link between our mental and emotional processes is cut. Probably because of establishing a self-image as adults, we rarely let loose the expression of these emotions with full impact so that the process can be therapeutic as in laughing, groaning, and wailing. Therefore it would be of great value to induce these emotionally cleansing sounds. We do not need to wait for moments of great emotion to sweep over us to receive their therapeutic benefit (see chapter 8).

The highest form of healing vibrations using the voice lies in toning and chanting. These have a greater power than singing, healthful as this is, because composers do not attempt to focus their unfolding patterns of sound to have definite therapeutic effects on those singing the sounds, much less on the listeners. The limitation of singing in this respect is that music is continually changing its patterns and is often full of contrasts—the rising and falling of the vocal lines, the changing of keys, and the ever-changing rhythms, dynamics, and text. Imagine the power, however, of many repetitions of just one phrase from J. S. Bach's *Mass in B Minor* given time to enter deeply into the singer's body, mind, and spirit. This is what occurs in toning and chanting in which the sound formulas are extremely concentrated and repetitive, allowing them the time and space to fulfill their purpose.

The subtle and powerful vibrations that can be produced by the human voice serve as an ideal resonating force for stimulating, purifying, and balancing the energies that generate wholeness—the integration of body, mind, and spirit. All aspects of vocal sound—speech, natural sounds, singing, toning, chanting, and overtoning—can contribute to this process. Unlike all manner of electronic instruments that are employed as sound therapy, the voice is always with us wherever we go and we have conscious control of how it will be used. It allows us to be our own natural sound healers. Such vocal soundwork requires only a modicum of instruction to be effective. Applied with knowledge and directed with intent, the voice can be a potent means of healing ourselves.

Integral to the application of therapeutic vocal sound is language, the combination of vowels and consonants that form what we call "words" to which meaning has been given. The biblical story of the tower of Babel tells us that in the beginning there was only one language and then the peoples were scattered and became separated from one another, each group establishing their own language. It is doubtful that we will ever know what this "original" language was and how it evolved. Perhaps the closest we can come to it, especially if it was a sacred language, is Sanskrit, the language of the religious scriptures of Hinduism still being toned today. Whatever the evolution of the many languages on Earth, a principal question remains: Does each sound formula or "word" equate vibrationally with the action or object it describes? Is the relationship arbitrary? Is it the intoning of the sound that gives it meaning or is the word's meaning inherent even without being set into vibration? If words are first and foremost vibratory constructs setting up particular resonances, what effects are they having on our energy fields? In this respect, what is the relationship of the primary vowels to the secondary consonants? In considering these questions, contemplate the sound of your own name because, in essence, it has no meaning. Yet it is a sound formula that has somehow come to embody who you are, and as we become familiar with our character, we might even alter the sound of our name or change it entirely. Ancient sacred traditions held that to know the true name of a person is to have power over that person. We can also have an awareness that language is a series of sound formulas when we listen to a foreign language that we do not understand. We perceive it as we would abstract music and revel in its sound.

As you engage in the sound rituals of toning, chanting, and over-toning, you will develop a taste for the character, frequency levels, and resonance capacity of the vowels and consonants and discover how they affect you. For example, in the consonant R there is an undeniable dynamism and fire that can stimulate the abdominal region of the body. The Hindus associate the R sound with the element of fire and the active force which they call *Rajas*. Whereas the M sound, the antithesis of the R, has an inner-directed, passive vibration as in humming, primarily felt in the head. Similarly most would feel that the sound of AH represents awe and wonder emerging from the heart region. The vowels are the carriers of languages and link closely with our feelings. The consonants modify the flow of the vowels in various ways and relate more to the mental plane. Consider how much the movements of the tongue are involved in order to create the consonants compared to the vowels.

It is essentially the strongly applied vibrations of the vowel/consonant system that enables the voice to be a resonating instrument for the fine-tuning of the physical body, the mental faculty which we call "mind," and other aspects of the energy field surrounding the body. This, in turn, releases a special energy, quite different from raw physical energy, which the Hindus refer to as *Sattva*—the energy of being. When such resonances touch upon all these dimensions, then the word *healing* becomes truly applicable. The root meaning comes from the

Old English word *hal* and translates as "whole," that is, perfect health. It is separate from *cure* which means to eradicate permanently an illness lodged in the body or mind. In dealing with the lepers, Jesus implicitly made a distinction between a cure and healing. Of the ten lepers who were cured, only one returned to Jesus and praised God because he had become whole and therefore truly healed (Luke 17:12). Despite the full self-realization of two well-known spiritual teachers of India, Ramana Maharshi and Ramakrishna, they were still subject to the physical laws of the body and died of cancer. When Ramana Maharshi was asked if he felt pain, his answer was "yes," but he also said he did not experience the mental attachment of suffering. Each of us has a particular set of physical body circumstances and there are no guarantees that anything will stave off disease.

So it is fairly unlikely that the application of therapeutic vocal sound will cure any life-threatening diseases or remove serious mental health problems. What it can do at the physical level is alleviate or even dispel stress and symptoms of various ailments: headaches or upset stomachs, for example. Or it can stimulate the glandular system to help the body fight off infections, calm the nervous system when it is under the strain of an illness, or release energy blockages situated in different regions of the body, so that, for example, constrictions in the throat could be undone, allowing a free flow of communication in speech. At the mental level it can ease anxiety when undergoing the various pressures of daily living. Its greatest practical application lies in preventative health by keeping our bodies, visible and invisible, in good tone and vibrating at all the correct rates. Then we would have the following benefits that lead to "healing," a state in which body, mind, and spirit are perfectly integrated:

1. Physically, the cells, the glands, the organs, and the circulatory system would be operating with complete efficiency. The nervous system would be functioning under less stress and consequently the whole body would find itself in a state of relaxation and breathing would be unrestricted.

2. Mentally, a stability and clarity of mind and an expanded awareness would be established. At the same time emotions would become purified and free from negativity. The rhythmic patterns of the body and mind would be integrated.

3. Spiritually, there would be experiences of unconditional love and happiness and of a sense of oneness with all living things and objects.

Complements to the Resonating Voice

SILENCE AND MEDITATION

It has been said that the canvas on which music is created is silence; that it emerges from silence and dissolves back into silence. This second silence is far greater than the first because, by the end, the music has built up its great archetypal form within the space and in its wholeness it remains suspended for the audience to continue to live in its presence. In some ways this final experience after the music in its aural form concludes is greater than that which preceded it. That is why it is wrong from a spiritual point of view to applaud music. The irregular noise of clapping hands disperses completely the fine energy form that the music has established and which the audience can actually feed upon. This is also why music in recorded form, as much as it is a blessing in some ways, can never duplicate the live musical phenomenon. The recording cannot capture the aura-like energy field that is generated by the music and its interrelationship with the minds of the audience, nor can it maintain it once the music is over. In India, for example, audiences will show their appreciation for a classical music performance by waving their hands in space so as not to disturb the special atmosphere created by the *ragas.*

This is also true for the creation of healing vibrations. The first few moments of silence as you prepare and collect yourself in order to focus your intention are important. In that beginning silence we hear the sounds within that in a moment will be sounded without. We may also be directing where we want the sounds to go. You could take up to 30 seconds before producing the audible sounds.

As in the ideal performance of music without applause, so the silence that follows our vocal sound rituals is far greater than the preparatory silence. First of all, physically we need to have rest after using our voices with great intensity for 10 or more minutes. At the same time, this latter silence becomes a form of meditation that can be held anywhere from 5 to 30 minutes. These are moments of centering and assimilation in which we can have direct experience of what the sound ritual has achieved, usually and most notably a complete sense of physical relaxation, a quiet pulsation of energy that feels like pure love, a great clarity of mind, and a deep serenity of spirit. The creation of healing vibrations is the prelude to the succeeding, profound state that is meditation. No matter what your motivation for using therapeutic sound, ultimately you come to recognize its natural endpoint in the meditative act. In this respect the process of vocal sound leading towards silence and meditation relates closely to the mantra yoga tradition of India wherein the aspirant is given sacred seed syllables to repeat inwardly until they go so deep into the consciousness as to become just a rhythm before disappearing altogether.

Relevant to therapeutic sound as a process that can open up a higher state of consciousness beyond our usual state of psychology is the scientific research[1] that has established four states of consciousness based on the measurement of our brainwaves. As the wave forms (in terms of cycles per second) decrease, our minds increase their capacity to be intuitive and even psychic.

FOUR STATES OF CONSCIOUSNESS

Beta

This is the level that all human beings experience as they go about their daily lives. It has little potential for fine creative work or thinking. It just gets us through each day performing various jobs and engaging in many activities. It is very active when we are in states of tension and fear.

Alpha

At this next level the ordinary, formative-thinking mind is disengaged, allowing us to enter into the first stage of meditation. The production of these brainwaves creates a state in which we are both relaxed and alert and begins to open up the channel for creative thought and artistic work.

Theta

This third level is equivalent to the deepest state of meditation at the point where one might slip into sleep. If this state of deep silence and peace is reached and maintained for even a few minutes, the potential for the release of very refined creative energy is enormous.

Delta

These waves are the slowest and place us in deep dreamless sleep in which we find fundamental rest. However, because we have no awareness in this state, we are unable to tap the experience of the union between ourselves and the universal consciousness.

Through the application of healing vibrations in the form of toning, chanting, and overtoning our state of consciousness can be shifted out of the Beta mode into at least the Alpha and perhaps even the Theta mode.

In all the sound rituals outlined in the succeeding chapters, you are urged to engage in some form of silent meditation at their conclusion.

Those who already practice a form of meditation should naturally enter into it. Those who do not can choose from the following procedures according to what best suits their nature. Silent meditation is usually done sitting down and needs good posture.

POSTURE

Sit in a straight-back chair without slouching, feet planted firmly on the floor, arms relaxed and hands, with palms up, resting comfortably in your lap or the right hand lying in the left. If the Yoga lotus position is familiar to you, then use it by all means. It is important to have an upright back so as not to impede the flow of energy as it rises from the base of the spine. If you are physically incapacitated and cannot maintain an upright position, then assume a lying-down position.

FOCUS OF ATTENTION

Attention in meditation means a steady state of awareness, not overactive concentration in which there is some special effort of will. Naturally, as it is about inner experience, it will be done with eyes closed. In the first instance, you will inwardly follow the sounds you have been doing aloud. This means decreasing the volume of the sound to the point where its repetition is only within your mind. Continue to shape the sound in the vocal cords, even though they are no longer active. Follow the sound as it turns eventually into a rhythmic form. Beyond this state all is silence.

Alternatively, the sounds made outwardly can be discontinued as they reach their quietest level. Then focus your attention at the base of the spine. It is possible that you will sense, arising from that point, a throbbing or pulsing that is neither your heartbeat nor your breathing. It is like discovering your natural mantric sound that was lying dormant there, waiting to be awakened. This is the sound of the energy flow itself. The other choice of focus is your breathing which becomes deep and evenly rhythmical after the soundwork. For example, it is perfect for the mantric chant "Soham" which is done slowly and evenly on the breath (see chapter 10). However, if the soundwork has been vigorous as in laughing or is accompanied by strong movements, the rate of the breathing is increased. Rather than attaching yourself to that rate, it would be better to focus on the base of the spine as the lungs slow down.

During the meditation, thoughts, visual images, or colors might flash across your mental screen. Let the experience of the higher state of awareness induced by the soundwork keep your focus of attention so that you can stay detached from any possible thoughts, images, and colors. Then the fullness of the integration of body, mind, and spirit can be assimilated and later used. Colors are particularly attractive and are an indication of a transformed state. Nonetheless, the ideal is to go beyond them because there is a deeper state to be reached. How long you remain in meditation as a result of your soundwork is your choice. This can be anywhere between 5 and 30 minutes, depending on how much time you can allot to the balancing of sound and silence. Some people will find the silent state uncomfortable because they feel that they have lost touch with themselves, or to be specific, their ego. In fact, the opposite is true. The deeper the stillness the more you are in touch with your true self that, later on, can be tapped for all sorts of creative purposes. You must see what the experience is but, at the very least, allow yourself some form of silent pause as you end the soundwork.

MOVEMENT AND GESTURE

Movement is fundamentally complementary to the creation of sound as vibration itself consists of an initial pulsating force that then sends out actual waves. Creation is movement. When we engage in vocal sound— speech, natural emotional sounds, or singing—almost invariably gestures and bodily movements complement those sounds. It is as though the physical body, stimulated by the vibrations of the vocal cords, the source of the initial pulses, has to respond in some complementary way to add to the emotional impact of expression. Very few of us remain entirely motionless while the vocal cords, tongue, and lips are in motion. The exceptional ones are the great spiritual teachers who have great stillness of body when imparting their universal knowledge.

Movement and gesture encourage vocal soundwork to emerge with a greater intent, force, and direction, and ritualize the act of therapeutic sound, adding to its emotional impact. Also, the very loosening of our bodies helps the vocal mechanism to relax, reducing any constriction. Such movements do not have to be rigorous to produce a freer sound. They should be similar to the Eastern methods of movement known as T'ai Chi (meaning "the way of the one energy") and Chi-Kung (meaning "the cultivation of the one energy") and Eurhythmy (that includes vocal sound), devised and promoted by the universal teacher and seer Rudolf Steiner in the last century. Movements like T'ai Chi and Chi-Kung are executed slowly which imparts a feeling of timelessness, an expansion of the present moment that complements the repetition of the vocal sounds. They are harmonious and open up the channel for a fine energy flow. In a word, they are graceful, signifying not only beauty of form but also the strengthening of a person through the Holy Spirit.

Movement and gestures, in conjunction with intent and visualization, assist in directing vocal sounds to particular regions of the body and they allow those sounds and the breath to move freely. For example, if you want to resonate the heart energy center, you could place your hands on your heart, move them away from the body about six inches and then return them to the heart in rhythm with the toning or chanting. Such a movement would encourage the vibrations of your voice to gravitate towards the heart region. If the toning or chanting is continued inwardly as a mantra in preparation for meditation, the complementary movements can also be continued in silence, helping to perpetuate the inner rhythm established.

It is quite possible that you could develop your own intuitive movements and gestures with toning and chanting. Some form of optional movement and gesture in conjunction with many of the sound rituals will be offered and described in the later chapters.

VISUALIZATION AND TOUCH

Visualization is the power of the mind to direct the flow of energy to where it is needed. As toning is often focused towards particular areas of the body, visualization can assist in getting the vibrations of your voice to those areas and act as another tool for centering and grounding your being. The hands can then serve as extensions of the mind's visualization. Once you are engaged in soundwork, the energy flow is stimulated, especially to the hands which naturally acquire a healing touch. This is the basis of a well-known healing process of the laying on of hands called Reiki, which translates as "universal life energy." There is a natural interchange and circulation of energy between the vocal sounds, the hands, and the region of the body touched. To combine vocal sound with touch also adds to the emotional impact, giving the feeling that we are loving ourselves, not sensually but spiritually.

Toning and chanting and touch can also be combined within partnerships. One or both partners can receive the therapeutic touch from the other while both produce the sounds. This can be done simply by connecting each other's hands. Alternatively, the partner producing the sounds can place their hands near to a particular part of the body to be toned. At the same time the sounds can be projected into that particular area. If they desire, the person being toned can vocally join in the process as well. Assuming that there is mutual trust between the partners, such links can increase the power of the resonating voice. A specific application of touch is described in connection with the toning of the chakras (see chapter 11).

TUNING FORKS

With tuning forks, one must defer to the pioneering work of John Beaulieu who has designed such forks as a complement to his polarity therapy work. Toning can be combined with listening to pairs of these tuning forks, one for each ear, that are tuned to pure intervals—intervals derived from the natural overtone series. (See resources under "Selected Non-Vocal Therapies" for further explanation.)

5

Breath and the Resonating Voice

If the world is composed of nothing but an infinite array of vibrations spawned by the Word, exactly how was that Word initiated? Coming down to the microcosmic world, it is clear that we cannot produce any words without engaging the breath, the exhalation of the air element through the vocal cords. So then we have to conceive that even before the Word, there was breath, the life force itself, or *prana* as it is called by the Hindus, *chi* by the Chinese, *pneuma* by the ancient Greeks, and *ruach* by the Hebrews, who used this same word to mean "spirit." Breath is its own vibration and inseparable from the Word. In the sacred scriptures of India, the creation (outbreath) and dissolution of the universe (inbreath) are described as the "great breath." Even the words for this process, inhalation and exhalation, contain the root word *hal*, meaning "wholeness." Breath is not the mere taking in of oxygen and the release of carbon dioxide, a process we take for granted. The air we breathe is a living current of food that, like electricity, supplies a power to the body and the mind. A brain starved of oxygen is robbed of the life force itself and results in a vegetative state. Nowadays the dilution of oxygen in the air, due to increased pollution, is a root cause for all sorts of illnesses.

It is not just the physical body that breathes, but the mind and the spirit as well. The Bible tells us in Genesis 2:7 that, "The Lord God formed man of the dust of the ground, and breathed into his nostrils the breath of life; and man became a living soul." A comparison between the Sanskrit word *Atman* meaning "the divine, individual self" and the German word *atmen* meaning "to breathe," demonstrates how important the breath is as the foundation of our existence. This same root sound is found in the word *atmosphere,* a life energy for the planet itself. It is also significant that in the Tantra Yoga tradition, the element of air is linked to the heart center, the other sustaining organ of life.

It is not the purpose of this book to delineate any special science of breathing, such as pranayama, part of the discipline of Hatha Yoga. However, the breath, as the great initiator and supporter of steady, firm vocal sound, cannot be ignored. Practicing a simple form of breathing technique will not only improve the quality and length of sound but also suffuse your body/mind/spirit complex with a greater amount of that life current and living food known as air.

To produce sounds that have sufficient potency for healing work, it is practical to increase the lung capacity and the control of the abdominal muscles. In ordinary life, many people are shallow breathers because of either conscious or unconsciousness stress anxiety. Such tensions constrict the upper body and the intake of air is minimized. Where there is deep relaxation there is bound to be deeper breathing. Working consciously with breathing, with or without vocal sound, is a special process. It is not advisable, nor really possible, to have a conscious awareness of the breath while fully engaged in life. At those times we leave the breath to its own devices. However, breathing exercises designed to increase the duration of breath can carry over into your daily routines.

The key to the process, whether your air intake is through the nostrils or the mouth, is the diaphragmatic muscle that lies beneath the lungs. Its relaxation will enable you to open up your lungs to a greater extent and allow more air to be inhaled. This is easier said than done because we are not used to either relaxing or contracting our abdominal muscles. So the first step is to practice working with these muscles which, in turn, will allow the diaphragm to release the lungs for greater capacity of inbreath as well as expelling the outbreath.

Preparation for Breathwork

Before beginning actual breathwork and to get the abdominal muscles working, place your hands on the abdominal region so that they can act as a monitor. Next, relax the region. During this period continue breathing normally. Because this relaxation does not come naturally to many people, it is necessary to push out the belly quite consciously so it protrudes without straining. Then, conversely, very slowly contract the abdominal muscles as though you want the front wall of your belly to pass

through your back. Do this gradually each time and build up to it, as maximum efforts at an early stage can lead to strain. Return to the expanded belly position as soon as you have fully contracted the abdominal muscles, letting the muscles go quickly into the protruding position. This release of the abdominal muscles often causes air to rush naturally into the lungs. Allow about 15 seconds of breathing through the nose and following the breath before proceeding to contract again. Spend around 3 minutes doing this exercise each time before taking up the actual breathwork incorporating these movements.

A secondary preliminary exercise is the opening of the throat for producing unrestricted sound. It is very much like gargling where the objective is to get a liquid as far back into the throat as possible while pushing air against it. For this exercise three gargling-like sounds are used:

GING GANG GUNG

Shape the mouth as though it contains a round ball with the lips open wide. Do not stretch the jaw to where it feels tense. Keep the tongue completely still, sitting at the bottom of the mouth. Then, without moving the mouth or tongue, sound out each of the words above from the back of the throat. The shaping of the different vowels presented should come from deep within the throat as in gargling. They can be practiced in a short, steady rhythm either repeating one of the three over and over or moving from one to the others. Alternatively, after sounding one of them, allow the air to continue to flow through the throat and a humming sound is the result. Naturally this way will produce a slower rhythm. The important point is that these gargling sounds are pronounced, so to speak, not sung. However, the subsequent humming sound, if used, will be a note but that is separate from the original pronunciations.

Exercise for Opening the Throat

Pronounce each sound as described nine times (which could be divided into three sets of three using the previously described humming sound after each set) and then feeling that mouth position, tone the corresponding vowel sounds set out below. Take in a deep breath through the nose before assuming the mouth position. Allow any note to emerge, changing over the vowel sounds at the halfway point of the breath. At this point there is no particular procedure for your breathing and breath control. Later, when taking up the general instructions for breathing development, return to this exercise applying what has been suggested.

Sound	Vowel Sounds
GING (9x)	HOH - HOO
GANG (9x)	HAH - HAY
GUNG (9x)	HEH - HEE

This opening of the throat work can be accompanied and enhanced by movement. Stand with one foot in front of the other in a balanced position. The back foot is turned outward at roughly a 90 degree angle to the front. You may change which foot is in the front throughout the exercise. Place your hands in front of your mouth as though holding a ball of energy the size of the open mouth cavity. When sounding the vowels, push out the ball of energy, slightly leaning the body forward but not bending at the waist. At the halfway point with arms not fully extended, pull the hands away from each other, palms always facing each other so that the ball is still held, and with a rounded motion draw the hands back to their original position.

At the same time pull the body back from its leaning position. After the three sets of three, take a pause breathing through the nose and keeping attention to your breath.

For the purpose of therapeutic vocal sound, the intake of air will be through the mouth rather than the nostrils. Deep rhythmic breathing through the nostrils would be conducive to entering the meditative state because you are drawing the prana into the head region where it can contribute to the calming of the mind. Breathing through the mouth is connected with action, in this particular case the production of vocal sound. Also, there is less likelihood of muscular tension in the upper part of the body when easily taking in air through the mouth.

General Instructions for Breathing Development

Stand with your feet apart with knees well relaxed so that they are ever so slightly bent.* Feel well-balanced and as though you are deeply rooted to the floor. Place your hands lightly on the abdominal region. Keep your head straight and close your eyes for concentration. Remember to have a relaxed throat so that your tongue lies comfortably at the bottom of the mouth. Expand the belly to its fullest extent as described above. Now you are prepared for an inbreath.

Imagine that you have a very large glass of air with a straw in it. This straw is very long and it extends from the glass, past your lips and all the way down into the protruded belly. Your lips will have a small aperture shaped to make the sound of OOO (as in "food"). Now begin gently sipping in the air with a continuous light suction action. To draw in air in this manner requires the absolute minimum of muscular activity so that the throat can maintain its state of relaxation and the whole of the chest region

---

*Hereafter this description will be referred to as "the usual standing position."

need not be involved. You should not even hear the air passing inwards. Visualize that you are first gradually filling up and expanding your belly with air, layer by layer, as though you are a kind of balloon. Then keep adding layers into the chest cavity so that you feel well suffused with the pure spirit of air, especially as it touches your heart. During this inbreath the only muscles that are engaged are those needed to keep the belly expanded and those that allow the air to be sucked in. The limit to the inbreath is determined simply by the sense that you feel a fullness without engaging the muscles of the neck, chest, or shoulders. If you begin to constrict in these areas, then that is a signal to stop the intake.

The exhalation is done through the same shaped mouth aperture. Ever so slowly, contract the abdominal muscles as described in the preliminary exercise so that a steady, quiet stream of air emerges. Allow your hands to monitor the contraction without actually pushing on the area. With practice, the flow of air can last between 20 to 30 seconds. In the early stages of this practice, go back to normal breathing before embarking on the next cycle.

As the breathing technique develops you can begin to do continuous cycles of inbreath/outbreath without returning to your normal breath. In this instance, as soon as all your breath has been expelled without straining, allow the belly to be pushed out to its fullest extent and begin the intake directly. Strictly speaking, this is not rhythmic breathing because the duration of the inbreath and outbreath will probably be different. Traditionally, the two aspects are usually evenly divided so that, for example, you actually count a certain equal number of beats for each cycle, with the option of the breath being held halfway through. In this case, the rhythmic steadiness of the breath becomes a form of meditation. For our purposes the practice of increasing breath capacity and control is not towards such an end (although it might have this effect) but simply an aid to increasing the benefits of working therapeutically with vocal sound.

Variations on the Basic Technique

1. Instead of only the air emerging on the outbreath, make the sound of WHO, as in the sacred HUU of the Sufi tradition (see chapter 10), at a medium volume. The opening H helps the sound to begin. The mouth is already shaped to produce this vowel.

2. Add TH in front of the WHO. The TH requires that the tongue, slightly curled and with its tip behind the upper teeth, blocks the flow of air thereby causing the air to strike against the roof of the mouth. This has the added value of stimulating the head region. Do this forcefully, spending the first 5 seconds of the outbreath on the TH before moving to WHO. Feel it vibrating the head region and relate it to the English words THought and THink.

3. To enhance this breathing technique, include the following movements either with a silent outbreath or with the continuous sound of WHO:

   a. Start in the usual standing position. Begin by holding your hands together in a prayer posture at the level of your waist, the fingers pointing outwards. As you draw in air, slowly separate the hands sideways. Keep the fingers pointing straight ahead as though holding a ball. The stop point coincides with the completion of the inbreath. On the outbreath, imagine your hands to be a kind of bellows as you move them slowly back to the original position. Time this so that your hands join at the center of your body at the point where all your breath has been expelled.

   b. Start in the usual standing position. Have your hands at your sides. With the inbreath, raise your arms slowly to the sides. Have the elbows slightly bent as though you were a

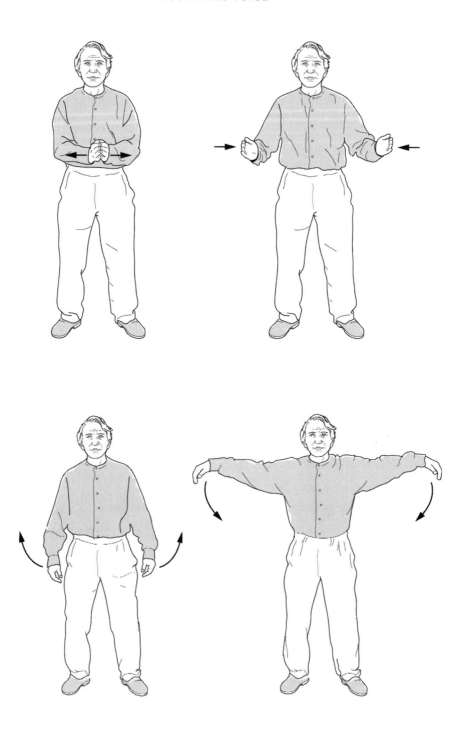

bird about to take flight. Have the wrists relaxed and the fingers curved so that when you reach the fully extended position of the arms, at least to the level of the shoulders, the fingers will be pointing towards the floor. Again, time this movement so that the completion of the inbreath matches the point where the arms are extended sideways without the elbows being rigid. On the outbreath, imagine the arms as bellows as they slowly descend back to the original position, timing this movement so that the breath ends when the hands reach your sides.

4. As an alternative to number 3, use the following movements and the sequence of vowels OO-OH-AH-AY-EE.

   a. Start in the usual standing position. Hold a ball of energy the size of an orange at the level of the throat just under the chin. As the inbreath is taken, pull the ball of energy down to your solar plexus. By this time the fingers are parallel to the floor. Now pull the hands away from each other as though expanding the held ball just past the width of the body. These two actions are to be done continuously with no stopping in between. Then, as in 3a, slowly push the hands towards each other as though there is a little resistance until the ball is again centered in front of the solar plexus. During the push sound out the vowels on any comfortable tone, sliding from one to the next and dividing them equally according to the estimated length of the breath. An added touch is to give a little extra abdominal push as the vowel is changed, a kind of mini-accent.

   b. Start in the usual standing position. Hold the hands with palms up and fingers pointing up and touching each other at the level of the throat. With the inbreath, let the hands descend along the body and at the solar plexus begin to pull them away from each other creating an arc-like motion in the process. As a matter of course the hands will fall below the level of the solar plexus. Allow the hands and arms to rise up without tension, as in 3b, until the arms are parallel to the ground. On the outbreath sound the vowel sequence as before and slowly push the hands down creating the arc-like motion in reverse. Let the hands come to rest on the body just below the solar plexus, the left hand resting on the right for women and vice-versa for men. Follow your breath through the nose and, when ready, slide the hands up to the original position and begin a new sequence.

The Cleansing Breath Exercise

This exercise combines the deep breathing technique with visualization and toning vowel sounds. The objective is to have the cleansing sensation of air pouring both up and down your entire body. The intake of the breath remains the same in this twofold process.

Step 1

Stand with feet shoulder-width apart and knees relaxed. Eyes closed. Extend your arms straight above the head with fingers pointing upwards. The elbows can be slightly bent so that the arms are not tense. Imagine your hands are embracing a column that is rising out of the top of your head. On the inbreath, draw your hands slowly downward so that first the palms pass in front of your face. As they continue on down, palms facing inward, the fingers will point toward each other at the heart and finally point downward as the hands reach the groin region. In this process you are not only visualizing pulling the breath down through the crown of your head as it fills your belly but also trying to sense

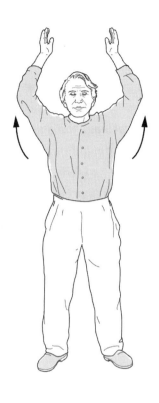

Hah

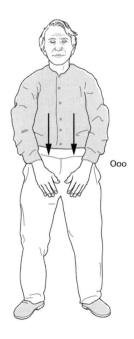

Ooo

your bioenergetic field or aura. This sensing will determine how far or near to your physical body your hands move. This could be between two to eight inches from the body. The speed at which the hands draw down the air depends on how quickly you feel saturated with air.

When the hands have reached the heart, release the air on HAH, using any mid-range tone. Slide the tone down five musical steps in a major scale (in musical syllables Sol Fa Mi Re Do),* changing the vowel sound to HOO as the hands approach the groin. Continue the HOO on the lowest tone until the breath runs out. Alternatively, remain on the same mid-range tone for both the HAH and HOO. At the end of this cycle breathe normally, and slowly move your hands upward reversing the movements until they are once again above your head touching the imaginary column. Do nine cycles.

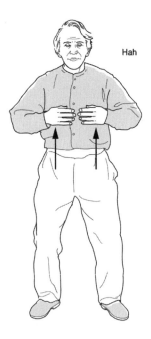

Hah

---

* Refer to chapter 7 where there is an outline of major scales. A good mid-range note would be D, the fifth note of the G major scale. In this case you would slide downward to G going through C, B, and A and upward to the upper G going through E and F#.

Step 2

Stand as before with a straight back but with the knees substantially bent. Eyes closed. Place your hands near to the groin as you begin your long inbreath. Visualize that you are pulling up the air from the soles of your feet through your legs and all the way up into the head. Let the hands rise accordingly. When they reach the heart with fingers pointing toward each other, release the sound of HAH on any mid-range tone and slide it upward four musical steps in the major scale (in musical syllables Sol La Ti Do). Change the vowel sound to EEE as the hands pass over the face and on up to the imaginary column. Continue the EEE on the highest tone until the breath runs out. Alternatively, remain on the same mid-range tone for both the HAH and EEE. At the end of this cycle, breathe normally and draw the hands down to the original position to start the next cycle. Do nine cycles.

6

Meaning of Vowels and Consonants

By establishing a correlation between vowel and consonant sounds, and their possible inner and outer meanings, the act of toning and chanting can be emotionally deepened, increasing substantially the benefits of soundwork. Think of all the vowels and consonants as pieces of fruit from which you want to extract as much juice as possible. The more pronounced and protracted they are, the more benefit you will receive. In all languages the vowels are the carriers. Our sentences ride on their wave forms. They are deep-rooted in us and in a sense they are the guts or bowels (vowels) of any language. In fact, the derivation of the word *vowel* relates directly to "voice."* The consonants are the consorts of vowels which, with their brief explosions, propel the vowels along. Only some of the consonants like L, M, R, S, W, and Z can actually be sustained. All the basic vowel sounds such as AH, OH, OO, I, and EEE

---

* The Latin word *vocalis* translates as "speaking and singing" but also means "vowel" when combined with *littera* meaning "letter of the alphabet."

are sacred in the sense that they are universal, have a purity of sound, and can be made without the use of the tongue. Only the mouth changes shape. They are pre-lingual simply because they do not require the tongue. The very word *language* derives from the Latin *lingua* meaning "tongue." Language comes into being when the tongue is used to modify vowel sounds and produce the consonants.

The following descriptions are intended to provide a bridge between the intellect and the emotions so as to enhance the toning or chanting of the various vowel/consonant combinations.[1] On this basis it is conceivable that a special language of sacred sound could be established through the joining together of vowels and consonants in new ways. (See chapter 11 on "Toning Seed Syllables.")

VOWELS

AH

The very glyph A is one of the primary geometrical shapes—the triangle representing the number three. The significance of threeness is that the introduction of a third force allows for the reconciliation of duality and polarity and serves as a harmonizing intermediary. This is reflected in the religious trinities of Father, Son, and Holy Spirit in Christianity and Brahma, Vishnu, and Shiva in Hinduism. Some of the most significant names for the supreme deity incorporate the AH sound—God (pronounced GAHD), BrAHmAH (Hindu), AHllAH (Muslim), AHwooNA (Aramaic), and JehovAH or YAHweh (Hebrew). The greatest intermediary of reconciliation and harmony is an unconditional love which is pure heart energy. This is the motive force behind all our actions but often, and quickly, becomes distorted by the dominance of ego. Therefore, this open vowel is associated with the heart, the very word in English sounding as HAAART. It is also the sound of wonder as when we witness something AHWE inspiring. When AH is sounded the mouth is at its widest as though all possibilities exist within it. AH has a dynamic energy that moves outward in all directions. As it is the first letter of the alphabet, it becomes the initiator. It is for this reason that we use the first Greek letter ALPHA as representing the beginning. Even the well-known OM sound of the Hindus begins with A when given in its Sanskrit form of AUM. Related to this is the Western Christian mantra AH MEN, which is also one of the names given to the one Creator in ancient Egypt.

AW

This vowel sound has a gripping and wrenching quality that can be connected with our will and hence to the solar plexus region. It buzzes with rich overtones and can SAW through blockages in that region. A most basic word beginning with this vowel sound is OUGHT, a word that implies duty not necessarily linked to willingness or love. So the feeling of "I ought to do this" is often accompanied by a tightness or knot in the abdominal area. This leads to being WROUGHT with guilt or OVERWROUGHT or DISTRAUGHT with stress. It is simply AWFUL, sometimes to such an extent that tears are produced and we BAWL. It is the sound naturally produced when we feel anger or frustration. We are blocked up as in the expression coming up against a WALL. Instead of being free we are ruled by the letter of the LAW. And this GNAWS at us and we can feel our character FLAWED.

AY

The AY sound is one of communication and can be associated with the throat region. The principal word association is with SAY but equally with the slang greeting of HEY. A significant word is OBEY whose root meaning is "to listen to your inner voice." This goes hand in hand with PRAY, to communicate with the higher worlds and PLAY, our free and joyous interaction with others. Communication is about making connections, of finding the WAY through, as it were. Conversely, when communication is colored by negative emotions, we PREY upon others.

EEE

This vowel has the highest rate of vibration or frequency and can be linked to the head region and beyond. In the Hindu tradition the vowel is associated with the highly active force known as *Rajas*. It is a sound that can catapult you beyond yourself and lead you into EEETERNITY or into EEEVIL if there is wrong intent. It is the great animator as in our English word KEEN. It is the vowel sound that stimulates you to act and go forward as in EEEmotion, EEEmanicipate, and EEEmerge. To wake up and BEEE, to find the KEEEY to life, and SEEE beyond the veils. In English we regularly refer to each other and ourselves as active, animated beings through the pronouns HEEE, SHEEE, WEEEE, and MEEEE. So revved up have younger generations become that many now start with the word ME when referring to themselves and another person—"ME and Robert" rather than "Robert and I." When we are frightened, our screaming often takes on the EEE sound, or when we are sorrowful and express our GREEEF, we begin to WEEEP.

EH

This is the short E vowel sound that is felt very much in the throat, the center point of our outward communication and expression, the latter word beginning with EH. It is the counterbalance of the heart (AH) sound as it is linked with the head, containing the sound of EH. It can be used in the throat region to break up rigid patterns there. Hence the past tense of "say," SAID. It is part of two of our most communicative words—HELLO and HELP.

EYE (I)

This is a significant vowel sound inasmuch as it refers in English to our egos, our I-ishness. The capital I, with its two short horizontal lines and one long vertical line, symbolizes that we are both a unity and a duality. In short, it stands for our ego and sense of Individuality. Even the

words which refer to our egos claiming ownership contain the I sound—
MY and MINE. To achieve integration between ego and the true self we
need INSIGHT, to see the greater reality of unity lying behind the illu-
sion. For this we need LIGHT and ENLIGHTENMENT. One of the
questions we ask in order to wake up to the greater reality is, WHY?
Then we are using our MIND wisely. This is the function of the so-called
"third eye," or brow chakra, which can be stimulated by the I sound.

OH

This is a companion sound to AH as both have the connotation of
embracing all possibilities within the creation. Both use a wide, round
mouth with a relaxed tongue to be sounded. Both can be expressions of
wonder, surprise, and discovery. As a glyph it is the symbol of unity, the
never-ending line going round. Visually and psychologically it represents unity and centeredness. First and foremost it is the sound of the
great Hindu seed syllable OM from which come the Latin-derived
words meaning both "all" and "everywhere"—OMNIPOTENT and
OMNIPRESENT. It also gives a deeper meaning to the place where we
feel centered and secure—HOME. The OH sound, as connected with
the solar plexus region, is also about positive creative tension and the
increase of inner strength. A warrior, summoning up his courage, might
GO forward to meet his FOE while chanting repeated HOs from his
belly. A seaman, needing extra strength to pull a rope, will shout out
"Heave Ho." Even Santa Claus, with his traditional pot belly, expresses
this sort of energy when he bellows out "Ho, Ho, Ho." There is no better example of creative tension than the string on a violin. It is only by
being stretched and made tense that it can produce a TONE, from the
Greek *tonos* meaning "tension."

OOO

This vowel, as in the word "food," is most clearly of the element water
when it flows steadily and gently in a stream. It literally OOOzes along.

It is connected with the sacral region of the body, the place of the woman's WOMB. This region is linked to our sexuality and hence to sensuality, as we find in such words as SOOTHING, WOOING, and COOING. At another level it is the creative force itself as in to DO and make something NEW.

The mystics of the Islamic tradition known as Sufis have identified this vibration of OOO with the Godhead, the ultimate Creator. For them HOOO is one of the sacred names of God. Their ecstasy in sounding out this sacred name is that of desiring union with the Supreme Being. In an unconscious way we identify ourselves with this Being when we ask others, "wHOOO are you?" or ask philosophically, "wHOO am I?" Turn these around and they become statements, "You are who" and "I am who." Through the sound of OOO we can acknowledge that we contain a divine spark and are therefore linked to the Creator.* Complementary to this is the word YOU, all the more significant by beginning with the heart-centered Y sound. This becomes more apparent when the two syllables HOOO and MAN are joined together into "human." In the word *human,* God (HOOO) is linked to our power of reason and discrimination; *manas* (man) from the Sanskrit means "mind."

CONSONANTS†

C/K

The glyph K (also the hard C sound) gives the image of a target being struck by an arrow. Just as an arrow pierces its target, so too the K sound can cut (Kut, also as it relates to Knife with its silent K) through energy blockages. It can send a shock wave down the autonomic nervous system as it hits the back of the neck and stimulate the glandular

---

* In the book *Talking With Angels,* transcribed by Gitta Mallasz (Daimon Verlag, 1988), the word for the one Creator is actually a sound O with an umlaut pronounced as OOO as in "lute."

† The choice of consonants has been made by their more frequent use in sacred sound traditions.

system in the process. There is a waking-up call (KALL) in this consonant. For example, the order of Middle Eastern dervishes known as the Mevlevi represents a call to "wake up and be" by the sound of KUM in their traditional whirling ceremony. The ancient Mayans of Mexico, in acknowledging the one Creator, used the K sound ritualistically in the seed syllable K'IN (see chapter 10 for a description of this chant).

The K sound can play a role in c(K)leansing (clean singing) our nature so that we can become fully c(K)onscious beings. It is about having a Key to unloCK the energy that leads us into higher consciousness. Its power is such that even when not sounded, it can thrust us into the Now. Thus, it signifies a deeper meaning in the words (K)now and (K)nowledge. Such energy leads us, in religious terms, to the Kingdom of heaven. Just as C(K)hrist, also referred to in the Greek as Kyrie (Lord), allowed Himself to be sacrificed on the c(K)ross—the ultimate act of love—so we apply things sac(K)red in order to exude that energy called "love." In order for this transformation to take place, we have to act with sufficient Keenness and Kindness. If we misuse the K energy we become c(K)aught, c(K)ritical, c(K)rippled, and c(K)razy and we c(K)rack, c(K)rash, and c(K)rumble. At the worst there comes c(K)rime and Killing.

H

H is the most spiritual of the consonants, connected as it is so deeply with our breath which regulates the influx of that life energy known in Indian philosophy as prana. Turn H on its side and it becomes I. It was pointed out that the I represents poles of duality joined together. If the duality in us is not balanced and reconciled into unity (the central line) then we feel pulled in different directions and cannot feel any centeredness. In other words, the breath sound of H is an antidote to the feeling of dispersion and separation. Interestingly enough, when H and I are placed next to each other, we have the sound that signifies a sense of expanding consciousness as in the expression "I feel high," rising upward and becoming lighter. Nowadays we are hearing more people greeting each other with "Hi" rather than "Hello." In either case this greeting is actually one of Honor as "Hello" comes originally from the word *Hallow*. By sounding a variation of "hallow" you are acknowledging the divine spark in another person, their Holiness and WHoleness. In the Tantra Yoga tradition, the H is connected with the throat, our center of communication from where these greetings are expressed. When the throat is blocked, we say that we are Hoarse. What we sound out in this region is the result of what we Hear from our earliest days. If we really Hear, then we are present or Here in the greatest sense. Without real listening there can be no true communication.

So many words of great power and emotion start with the H breath sound. To begin with, the two essentials of ourselves—Head and Heart. Here it is significant that the throat (the word contains a strong H element) is the link and halfway point between these two. When these are absolutely in balance, our natural wholeness becomes evident. And it leads to Hope, Happiness, Humility, Honesty, Harmony, Healing, and even Humor and creates Heroes and Heroines who can scale the Heights. Then we become fully Human (addressing people as Him and Her) and sing our Hosannas and Hymns and our spiritual Hunger is satisfied. The Harvest is ours. We know deep contentment and Hug and Hum to all beings. This state of affairs is the true Home for us. Like all sounds, the H can be misused and this is seen in the opposites of Heaven and Hell (Hades) and Help (including a Helping Hand) and Harm/Hate/Hardness/Hostility/Hunt/Horror/Harshness.

L

The glyph L is two lines at right angles, 90 degrees. In astrology it is equivalent to the square aspect which causes a strong vibrational effect in the form of challenges to the status quo. In the language of the Mayans the word *lil*, which was often reduced to the single sound of L, meant "vibration" in the cosmic sense. They preceded it with the sound of O, and as "OL" it meant "awakened consciousness in the form of vibration."[2] It was their equivalent to the Hindu OM. The Tantra Yoga system places the L vibration at the root chakra (linked with the element of Earth) from which our fundamental vibration and basic energy emanates—the seat of the Kundalini energy as identified by the Hindus. Coincidentally, this region of the body is called the Lumbar whose opening sound corresponds closely with the Tantra Yoga seed syllable for the root chakra—LAM.

The formation of the L as the tip of the tongue touches the roof of the mouth performs a vital energy function. According to Taoist healing tradition, there are two energy channels in the body, each beginning at the perineum. The Yin channel travels up the front of the body and terminates at the tip of the tongue. The Yang channel moves up the back of the body into the brain before finding its endpoint at the roof of the mouth. Consequently the sound of L acts as a trigger linking the two channels and causes a circular energy flow.[3]

A very significant word in English beginning with L is Love, which many great spiritual teachers refer to as the ultimate motivating force and vibration of the universe. This special impulse of love lies at the very root of us. However, the energy is easily diverted for selfish purposes and, for example, can turn to Lust. The other great force in our existence, and complementary to Love, is Light, consisting of the highest vibrations we can knowingly perceive. In these there is the very essence of Life itself. Humanity creates yet another force of vibration to express its experiences—Language which, in spoken form, is sound to which we Listen. For true listening, as when we perceive our inner voice, is a spiritual act. The strong vibrations of L through these essences, as well as such activities as right Learning and Laughter, can Lead us to spiritual freedom—Liberation.

Perhaps the most profound religious use of L is in the Muslim word for God—ALLAH—in which the L sound is strongly vibrated, uplifting the tongue deeply into the palette as in the word *lullaby*. Therefore "Allah" suggests the meeting of Heaven—the world of God, the vowel AH—and Earth—the world of man and the Land, the consonant L. This sound also connects directly with the Christian mantra "Alleluia." To this can be added the Christian religious words Lord (God), Lamb (of God), and Lent (the lengthening of the Light in spring).

R

The sound of R resonates with particular potency and, at the beginning of a word, tends to propel its sound forcefully. This consonant, more than any other, is about the fire element within us. The Hindus associate it with the attribute they call Rajas, that which initiates and sets an action in motion. In Western terms a rajasic person is one who is regularly hyperactive and overheated. We find it at the beginning of such fiery words as Roar, Roast, Riot, Rage, Rip, Race, Rampage, Rupture, Racket, Rankle, Raid, Ram, Rant, Ransack, Raw, Revolt, Rob, Robust, Rough, Rout, Rude, Ruin, Run, Rush, and all those words which use RE at the beginning meaning "to go at it again and again." When we were told to roar like a lion as children, invariably we chose the sound ERRRR. When cheerleaders in the United States want to fire up the spectators at a match, they use one basic sound—RAH. Little do they realize that subconsciously they are getting the crowd to worship one of the ancient Egyptian gods, Ra. And when we feel coldness of body, we sometimes send out the sound of BRRR in an attempt to light some sort of inner fire and warmth.

Two very important deities in the Hindu tradition are BRahma, the supreme creator being, and Rama, who endows men with courage through the strengthening of their physical, mental, and spiritual dimensions. In Tantra Yoga the sound for the solar plexus region, which certain traditions of the Far East consider to be the source of *Chi* energy and hence of determination and courage, is RAM. The spiritual implication of the fiery R sound is the burning desire within the heart to know union with God and is seen in such words as Religion, Righteousness, Rite, and Ritual.

M

This consonant is, above all, about feeling or conveying deep contentment as it is heard in humming, a sing-song prolongation of the MMM sound, or an affirmation and acknowledgement when sounded as "Mmmm" in short bursts. It also bespeaks the innocence and purity of the child who early uses the M in the form of "Ma Ma." To sound the MMM is to identify with the feminine energy that gives birth to the Material world, from the Latin *Mater* meaning "Mother." When we claim ownership of that material world, we use the MMM words of My, Mine, and Me. Because it can be easily produced with the mouth closed it feels very inner directed and has the attribute of passivity in the best sense of letting go, allowing, and surrendering, as found in the word May—to give permission.

In the spiritual traditions of both East and West it is found at the end of many sacred sound formulas. Two well-known examples are OM and A-Men. In closing our lips to produce the M, we realize that it is about a drawing inward and completion. Within Eastern traditions of meditation the M sound is linked to our slowest brain waves, Delta waves, which are equivalent to the deep sleep state. Within the Vedic teachings it is said that the actual sound of the real Self is MMM. Hence to sound the MMM is to come closer to who you really are. It naturally vibrates the upper chest region, the seat of the Soul, or can be pushed upward into the head region through a smile. It can calMMM and soothe (as in the word "balMMM") the Mind, especially where it is part of a Mantra. The sound of M encapsulates a spiritual energy that is integral to the act of Meditation and Mediation, to the application of true Medicine and Magic and to listening to Music. It contributes to Magnifying our consciousness and to becoming Masters of our fate.

S

This consonant is a sound representation of the life force itself, or Spirit. It enlivens, inspires, purifies, and nurtures intuition. It generates warmth and heat just as does the Sun, the basic life force for Earth. The Sun with its solar winds is like a radiator with its hissing. The sound of the word Sun can also be spelled as Son, the French word and the root for the word Sound itself. This connects with the word *person* through the Latin *per sonare* meaning "through sound." The whole basis of using the resonating voice is that we are "through sound" beings, a multitude of frequencies.

Two very essential religious words beginning with the S sound are Soul and Spirit. The soul holds within it the essence (note the double SS) of our nature and its purification leads to our becoming who we really are. The spirit is the divine influence (the Super, the Supreme, or the Source) that enables the soul to be a perfect agent for our actions, then we feel in complete Sympathy (as in "compassion") with the world. Along similar lines can be added the words Serenity, Silence, Stillness, Sacred, Sacrifice, Sanctity—meaning "to make holy," and Savior and Saint—holy ones. Yet any fine energy associated with the S sound can be misappropriated, hence such words for dark forces as Satan, Sorcerer (who casts Spells), and Sinister.

The S sound is particularly associated with the mental plane and its link to the Senses. Our most active sense is Sight operating at the levels of body, mind, and spirit. Beyond the physical sight we have our Subtle body, pSychology, Sanity (an ordered mind), inSight, and, at a deeper level, all pSychic phenomena. What appears in the mental is often transmitted through Speech (Saying) and Singing. For example, the Soothsayer, the one who speaks the truth.

As a glyph it is both a serpent when seen upright, and when seen on its side a wave, the form through which sound travels. In the Hindu tradition the fine energy source, or Kundalini, is known as the Serpent energy lying at the base of the Spine which can uncoil and rise up through the chakras. In the act of meditation the complementary states of Sound and Silence become one. The great symbol for this is the caduceus found in certain spiritual traditions throughout history and long associated with the healing arts.

Y

In the glyph of Y there is the symbolism of the one splitting into the two—the unity of the Absolute Being creating a universe of opposites, polarity and duality. This play of opposites is described in Chinese philosophy by the two Y words—Yin (feminine) and Yang (masculine). It is like a tree, the trunk giving way to the branches that reach out to the sun and the heavens. A worthy spiritual aim would be to reconcile the opposites and live in a world of non-duality. Such an aim has its focal point within the heart. The open, loving heart affirms life in all its apparent dualities. It says, "Yes" and "Yea," or in German *Ja*. The heart Yearns for union (literally, Yoga) with Oneness and gladly Yields itself. In the Tantra Yoga system the seed syllable for the heart is YAM. Within Western religious traditions there are the figures of Jehovah or Yahweh and Jesu (pronounced Yaysu), or Yeshua. Above all are the words which direct us most personally with one another, You, Ye, and Your(s). When someone says, "I am yours," it most often means a loving surrender from the heart.

V

The consonant V is about a potency of energy, a Vitality, Vim, and Vigor. In sounding it you hear and feel on your lips a wonderfully buzzing sensation. It is the essence of Vibration and at its source is the Voice, as it originally emerged into the Void. In the Tantra Yoga system the sound VAM relates to the sacral chakra, the seat of sexual energy sometimes described as Virility in men. This chakra is linked with the element of Water (and the related words Wave, Well, Wet, Wax/Wane, and Wade), which comes from the German word Wasser, the W (two Vs joined together) sounded as a V. This is also the region of the Woman's Womb. In these analogies V and W are taken as complementary sounds, the V projecting more vibration. In this way the words Virgin and Virtue, as they relate to both sexuality and purity, and Water, as a highly purifying agent, are implicitly connected. When sexual energy is repressed rather than transformed, it can turn to Violence, Vehemence, Vendetta, Vindictiveness, Vilification, Virulence, and Vice.

7

General Instructions for Toning and Chanting

WHEN?

The best time is in the morning before having breakfast. This is when you should be at a generally good energy level assuming you have had a good night's sleep. The toning and chanting will release a finer energy that can be used throughout the day. The rituals* can be taken up again in the early evening before a meal. This evening session can provide a way of relaxing the body and renewing depleted energy so that you can enjoy an engaging evening activity.

WHERE?

Preferably a room that is not used much, such as your bedroom or study, so that it feels to be your space. It is equally important that the

---

* Inasmuch as toning and chanting are the ritualization of sound, that is, sacralizing the sounds and giving them a greater depth of emotion, descriptions of them will often be referred to as rituals rather than exercises or activities.

room is not cluttered or filled with too many things and that there is a window to allow fresh air and sunshine, depending on the season, to enter. Spaciousness is conducive to the process. In keeping to the same room you saturate the space with good vibrations that give their own subtle impetus.

HOW LONG?

The length of time for toning and chanting can be variable. What is important is that the sound is balanced by silence, for this is the natural progression of the process. For example, you could do three sets of 5 minutes of toning and chanting followed by 10 minutes of silence, adding up to 25 minutes; or do a series of rituals lasting 15 to 20 minutes followed by the same amount of meditation; or do one for 10 minutes and meditate for a half hour. In the silence you can allow the sound patterns to continue inwardly for a time as in a mantra or use one of the other methods outlined in chapter 4 under the heading "Silence and Meditation." It is essential that you discover through experimentation what produces the best results.

WHAT TO WEAR

The main point to consider is that you do not restrict your breathing process by anything tight around the waistline. You want to be able to allow the belly to extend itself outwards as fully as possible. Naturally, you want to be warm and that will depend on your heating system. In the morning, some might choose to stay in their sleepwear while others would prefer to be dressed first.

How to Tone/Chant

1. The basic position for most of the voice work is standing with your feet apart, roughly under your shoulders, and your knees ever so slightly bent so that you feel grounded and relaxed. When no movements are used, have loose arms with hands at your side. Have a chair behind you so that you can sit down directly for the silent periods. If you have a problem standing, then by all means work from a sitting position. For sitting, you need a comfortable, straight-backed chair to support your back. Slouching of any kind will inhibit your sound. A few rituals, like the toning of the organs, actually require the sitting position.

2. Start with a short open throat exercise (see chapter 5) followed by some breath work for a few minutes. This gets your system activated. After that choose whatever sound rituals you like.

3. Hear the sounds within before intoning them and, if applicable, visualize where you would like the sounds to be located in your body. If no other instructions are given, place your hands lightly on the region where the sounds are to be directed. However, do not assume any uncomfortable positions such as putting your hands on the base of your spine.

4. Surrender yourself to the sounds, giving them an emotional purpose and intention. Let the desire for the release of healing energy be paramount. This attitude will coax from you a far more resonant sound. Produce the fullest sound possible without causing tensions in the body or being raucous. The intensity of the sound is more important than the length, for you can take in as many breaths as you like.

5. Close each ritual with a silent, meditative period.

FINDING NOTES

None of the rituals absolutely requires you to tone or chant on particular notes. However, fixing on a particular note is essential in discovering your fundamental tone. Also, in toning the chakras, one of the options is to follow a particular series of notes from a given fundamental tone. So it would be useful to have some source for obtaining these notes. The most readily available instrument is a small electronic keyboard which offers you a choice of twelve notes as each octave* is divided by that number. Electronic keyboards also have sounds such as the organ that can be sustained indefinitely, allowing the ear time to fix on a note. The notes of an ordinary piano die away as soon as they are struck. Other sources are a child's xylophone (not divided by twelve), a set of tuning forks (usually only a set of eight forks, one for each note of a major scale),† a harmonium (often used in Indian music), an electronic tuning device (used by guitarists for tuning), and a pitch-pipe.

KEYBOARDS

Nowadays electronic portable keyboards are four or five octaves in size. In either case, middle C, the note for orientation, is the third C up or two octaves higher than the low C, indicated in the following diagram. Also given are the names of all the white and black notes and, as a guideline, the ranges of men and women's voices. Note that the middle C of a piano is usually found under the name of the maker. It is the fourth C up from the bottom (starting on the left), the C to be found just to the left of a set of two black keys.

---

* An octave is the distance of eight consecutive white notes on a keyboard, going either up (to the right and getting higher in pitch) or down (to the left and getting lower in pitch). In moving in steps of eight you always return to the same letter note. Thus, starting from C, eight notes higher or lower is also C. The octave is divided into twelve degrees when the black notes are included, each step up or down, called either semi-tones or half steps.
† For example, those designed by John Beaulieu. See resources.

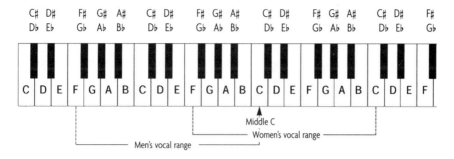

♯ - sharp

♭ - flat

Note: The vocal ranges are variable and correspond to bass and alto voices respectively. Nonetheless, there are enough notes encompassed by these ranges to do effective voice work.

DETERMINING YOUR VOCAL RANGE

This is optional and has some bearing on chants which use several different notes. Begin by producing any note spontaneously and match it by searching for the corresponding note on a keyboard. It could be a white or black key. For women, this will probably be near to middle C and for men, near to the C below middle C. Once you have made the match, move your finger downward (left), playing every white and black key in succession. At the same time, move your voice along with the notes played until your voice thins out. Go backwards to find the last note that has substance. This will give you your lowest note. Starting from the same note that you produced originally, move upward (right), note by note until your voice feels under strain. Go backward to find the last note where the voice feels free. This is your upper limit. A good range is ten to twelve white notes. However, a range of eight white notes will do. Most men and women can produce the range between G to G or A to A. For the women, this starts from the G or A just below middle C moving upwards, and for the men, starting from the same notes and moving downwards.

SCALE PATTERNS

Major

This is the traditional and fundamental seven-tone scale pattern of Western music and has been used by composers over roughly the last 350 years. The tones are often referred to by their syllable names of Do, Re, Mi, Fa, Sol, La, and Ti.

Overtone

The significance of this seven-tone scale pattern is that it is found naturally within the fourth octave of the overtone series (see chapter 12).

Pentatonic

This five-tone scale is the most universal and found in the music of many cultures, notably the Chinese. It misses out the fourth and seventh degrees of the seven-tone patterns. Its sound can be easily produced by playing only the five black keys of a piano keyboard from Gb/F# up to Eb/D# within an octave. It is the scale recommended for toning the chakras (see chapter 11). Note that in the twelve versions given, the first two notes are repeated an octave higher so as to correspond to the seven chakras.

The reason for presenting these three scales is to give choice, as teachers of therapeutic vocal sound suggest different methods for correlating tones with chakras.

The following are the major, overtone, and pentatonic scales beginning on each of the twelve notes within an octave. The sign # is called a sharp and the sign "b," a flat. These signs correspond to the black keys. Note in the diagram on page 61 that each black key has both a sharp and flat designation. The purpose of presenting twelve versions for each scale type is to allow you to begin with your own fundamental tone or to accommodate your particular vocal range. In the case of the major and overtone scales, the eighth note repeating the first an octave higher is given to complete the scale. However, only the first seven are needed for chakra toning.

MAJOR SCALES

C	D	E	F	G	A	B	C
D	E	F#	G	A	B	C#	D
E	F#	G#	A	B	C#	D#	E
F	G	A	Bb	C	D	E	F
G	A	B	C	D	E	F#	G
A	B	C#	D	E	F#	G#	A
B	C#	D#	E	F#	G#	A#	B
Db	Eb	F	Gb	Ab	Bb	C	Db
Eb	F	G	Ab	Bb	C	D	Eb
Gb	Ab	Bb	B	Db	Eb	F	Gb
Ab	Bb	C	Db	Eb	F	G	Ab
Bb	C	D	Eb	F	G	A	Bb

OVERTONE SCALES

C	D	E	F#	G	A	Bb	C
D	E	F#	G#	A	B	C	D
E	F#	G#	A#	B	C#	D	E
F	G	A	B	C	D	Eb	F
G	A	B	C#	D	E	F	G
A	B	C#	D#	E	F#	G	A
B	C#	D#	F	F#	G#	A	B
Db	Eb	F	G	Ab	Bb	B	Db
Eb	F	G	A	Bb	C	Db	Eb
Gb	Ab	Bb	C	Db	Eb	E	Gb
Ab	Bb	C	D	Eb	F	Gb	Ab
Bb	C	D	E	F	G	Ab	Bb

PENTATONIC SCALES

C	D	E	G	A	C	D
D	E	F#	A	B	D	E
E	F#	G#	B	C#	E	F#
F	G	A	C	D	F	G
G	A	B	D	E	G	A
A	B	C#	E	F#	A	B
B	C#	D#	F#	G#	B	C#
Db	Eb	F	Ab	Bb	Db	Eb
Eb	F	G	Bb	C	Eb	F
Gb	Ab	Bb	Db	Eb	Gb	Ab
Ab	Bb	C	Eb	F	Ab	Bb
Bb	C	D	F	G	Bb	C

8

Natural Sounds

When we were children we thought nothing of expressing our feelings through our voices without inhibition. We were doing what came naturally. When we were simply happy, we would play joyously and rhythmically with nonsense syllables. Perhaps they were not nonsensical but the remembrance of an ancient language known in a previous life or heard in the twilight world between lives. It is now documented that the first sense to develop in the womb is hearing and so we can be nourished not only by our mother's voice but also by any fine vibrations such as music that penetrate the mother's body. We are primed to make vocal sound at a very early stage in life.

There is such a wide range of natural vocal sounds, some caused by heightened emotions and others produced by the physical body such as yawning, sneezing, and belching. The key word here is *release,* allowing sound to be cathartic and so rid us of impurities that fester within, not allowing us to vibrate. For the vibrations of emotion can be turned into a medicine, shaking loose rigid patterns both in body and psyche. Such sounds are diffused through the body and even returned to it in circular fashion through the ears and the nervous system.

Emotions can be categorized easily as positive and negative but in working with sound as their expression or representation it is best to leave such divisions aside. Otherwise, it is easy to come to the conclusion that a clearly negative emotion such as anger should not be expressed. What is important is under what conditions and how we release emotions that relate, in one way or another, to the thwarting of the ego. If another person is involved in this feeling of thwarting, it must never be expressed in their presence because we have no way of knowing how they will handle the vibrations of the negative feelings. Even beyond the words, the sounds can cause disturbances in the balance of the psyche. Easier said than done, perhaps. If vocal sound is part of the release to rid yourself of this powerful thrust, then it has to be done privately. Later you can approach the other person and, having purged yourself, you can broach calmly and authoritatively whatever it is that caused the friction in the first place. Of course, if it is joy that is elicited by the other person, then you can, there and then, let the sounds of that emotion flow freely. Whatever emotion is released from you, it will have a far greater effect through pure vowel/consonant combinations than through ordinary speech. That is, if you were delighted at an absolutely beautiful scene of nature and could not contain your ecstasy, would it not be better to burst into song or just go, "Weeee, weeee, weeee" than tell yourself or another person again and again, "Look at that scene. Isn't it amazing!" Beyond the vocalization the even greater state, in this case, is silence, allowing the experience to saturate your being.

In working with natural sounds as part of a voicework program, you do not wait for situations to arise that produce emotional sounds. Regular conscious voicework will help to lessen and dissipate negative emotions in day-to-day life, if and when they do arise, and will allow the positive emotions to emerge more easily. As was noted in chapter 3 on having intent in projecting the resonance of the voice, it is important that you assume the role of an actor in natural sounds voicework. The more you can remember from past experience and conjure up the emotion that accompanies the sound the better. It adds intensity to the sounds that will increase their benefits.

In chapter 7, conditions are set out that are conducive to doing therapeutic soundwork. One of the recommendations is that it be done at the beginning of the day and/or at the end of the workday. However, this is not to say it could not be done at other times. Natural sounds, because they are about releasing emotions safely, can be put to use at any moment of your waking life when you feel the situation calls for it. So if feelings of depression, anxiety, anger, sorrow, or fear began to surface in you, you could put to use the soundwork to alleviate these conditions before they overwhelmed you. Of course, they would have to be done in private and it is understood that it is not easy to find such privacy at a public workplace. In this instance the practice of inner sound in the form of mantric chanting would take precedence (see chapter 10).

RITUALS OF NATURAL SOUNDS

Gibberish

One might not consider gibberish to be one of the natural sounds. Nonetheless young children are fond of playing with nonsense language and to that extent it is quite natural. They may well be practicing vocal sound therapy. In certain ashrams in India it is practiced as a way of getting out of our little self and to know the freedom of the greater self. It is an excellent beginning for a toning session, especially when working in groups. Being improvisational, it is immediately liberating and produces a wide range of vocal sounds in pitch, timbre, rhythm, and accents. For maximum benefit do it with exaggerated mouth and tongue movements, as well as arm and hand gesticulations. Produce the nonsense in different ways; for example, high and low, loud and soft, nasalized and whispered. In groups move about the space and converse in gibberish with different partners. The duration of a gibberish ritual is quite open ended. If it is a preliminary to a session and to get the juices of the voice moving, then 3–5 minutes is enough. If it is a main event, so to speak, each person can decide when they have had enough and collapse on to the floor in blissful exhaustion.

Yawning

Yawning is not connected with our emotions. Most of us associate it with tiredness, a running down of energy. It need not be accompanied by sound because essentially it is an involuntary action of drawing in a very deep breath. In yawning the body mechanism is trying to replenish the loss of energy. That is, the deep, sudden rushes of air are providing a quick fix of oxygen, the prana, revitalizing the whole system. Georges Gurdieff,[1] a well-known teacher of Eastern esoteric knowledge, taught that we have within us large and small energy accumulators that are interdependent, and yawning is a means of pumping energy into the small accumulators.

At the same time, yawning allows for the relaxation of the throat and tongue and the stretching of the jaw which makes it ideal as a preparation for toning, chanting, singing, and overtoning. If you really yawn, you have to open the mouth as wide as possible both for the deep intake and the release of air. It comes into the realm of natural sounds when you produce an AH on the outbreath, the AH forcing you to have a very wide and rounded mouth. The AH sound arising in the heart will also have the effect of undoing any tension.

So either you act out yawning deliberately when tiredness comes over you or when you want the mechanisms of throat, tongue, and jaw to be very relaxed prior to any voicework. In either case, it is a healthful thing to do.

Laughter

Whoever first said that laughter is the best medicine was responding intuitively to what has now been proven by the medical establishment. Through medical and psychological research it has emerged that laughter boosts the immune system through the release of an antibody, called immunoglobin, lowers the blood pressure, massages the heart, lungs, and other vital organs, stimulates the nerves, improves the body's use of oxygen, and gives relief to stress and depression. All of us have seen the

A Yawning Ritual

1. First practice opening your jaw as wide as possible while keeping a rounded mouth. Keep the jaw open for 5 seconds, imagining the sound of AH, and then close it slowly, keeping the mouth in the rounded position. Do this a few times before actually doing the yawning.

2. Now stand with your feet shoulder-width apart. Place your closed hands above your shoulders, facing forwards. Draw in air quickly and deeply through an ever-widening mouth, thrusting out your belly at the same time. Do not hold your breath. On the pushing out of the breath, make the sound of yawning. That is, produce a somewhat breathy AH sound from deep within your throat as though you were gargling, similar to the Ging-Gang-Gung exercise in chapter 5. At the same time stretch out the arms sideways and upwards as you would for a natural yawn and open up the hands. Do this with eyes closed. Hold this outstretched position for a few moments, breathing normally. Slowly draw the hands back to the original position. Do it anywhere between five and ten times.

---

transmitting power of laughter when one person's laugh sets off another for no apparent reason. In this we say that laughter is infectious.

There was the publicized case of the American publisher Norman Cousins, suffering from a severe form of cancer, who gave himself an intensive diet of funny films, books, and jokes that provoked laughter day in and day out. He was convinced that the daily dosage of laughter was the cause of the remission of his cancer. Dr. Patch Adams,[2] about whom a major feature film was made, uses and prescribes humor in all its forms for his patients. And in Birmingham, England, a laughter clinic was set up within the National Health Service under the direction of the holistic practitioner Robert Holden.

An interesting piece of research was done on the rates of laughter between youngsters and adults. The highest point was 300 laughs a day at age six; at adulthood, on average, it was about 47 times a day.[3] We can take life so seriously that we can fail to laugh at all on a given day. We would have more cause to laugh if we could see the absurdity of many situations in which we find ourselves or at least which we witness. Think of Dante Alighieri who had the wisdom to call his great masterpiece depicting three levels of existence *The Divine Comedy* and not *The Great Tragedy.*

The key to laughter lies in the sound of H. Even in our English language we see that H symbolizes laughter in the words *humor,* a word that also translates as "temperament" as in the four temperaments (melancholic, choleric, phlegmatic, and sanguine), and *hilarity.* (See chapter 6, "The Meaning of Vowels and Consonants.") Although there are many variants in the frequencies of laughter through the attached vowels, it is the initial H and how it is produced that causes its health-giving properties. We all know that if we laugh hard and long enough our sides begin to ache. That is because in order to produce a vigorous H sound, which is on the breath, we have to push those abdominal muscles. The H sound is the essential purifier as the breath is sent upward quite forcefully. As it does, it serves to stimulate the glands and the associated chakras along route.[4]

The basic laughter work is done by combining the breath H sound with five different vowel sounds that are directed to particular regions of the body. The rhythm of the laughter is usually steady but you are free to play with it in any rhythm you like as you would when laughing spontaneously.

Preliminary Exercise for Laughter

Stand with your feet apart, roughly under your shoulders. Place your hands on your sides at the waist. Take in a quick deep breath through the mouth, thrusting out and filling up the abdomen. On the outbreath do a series of rapid HUH HUH HUH HUH HUH HUH sounds, requiring you to tighten the abdominal muscles with each successive HUH. Feel this with your hands. When all the breath is expelled, take in another deep breath in the same way and repeat. If done vigorously, it is possible to experience a heat being generated in the upper parts of your body, even a burning sensation in the head. It is living proof that laughter is a living energy. This exercise can also cause light-headedness. This is a signal to discontinue the exercise. It will have shown you what the action of laughter is.

THE FIVE LAUGHTER SOUNDS

1. HUH as in the word HUG. It is the same sound as in the word LOVE. This is to be directed to the groin (or root chakra) and LUMBAR regions and base of the spine, the source of our energy. It is a deep, relaxed laugh and, as in all the laughter sounds, the mouth should be fairly open.

2. HOH as in the word HOLY. This sound is to be centered in your belly (or solar plexus chakra), the source of the Chi energy as described in Chinese philosophy. On the one hand, it is the sound of courage in a warrior's cry, determination in the seaman's call of "Heave Ho," and quest in the pioneer's cry of the American West, "Westward, Ho!"; on the other, it is the sound of jollity used to great effect by all those Santa

Clauses. Somehow Santa Claus, with his enormous belly, knows that his belly sound is HO and none other.

3. HAH as in the word HEART. This is the warmest of the laughter sounds as it emerges from the heart. Just as in the expressions of a "hearty laugh" or "they laughed heartily." This is the one we all know best and seems to go the farthest in tickling our funny bone.

4. HEH as in the word HEAVEN. In all the previous cases you have had to visualize the sound circulating in a particular area of the body as the frequency of the vowels increases upward. Here, they are one and the same as the HEH sound is used to stimulate the throat region. This region is about communication, and one of our chief words for immediate connection with others is HELP. This is the one laughter syllable that has the potential to sound sinister. So do not produce a strangulated sound in the throat. Keep it light and positive with a little breath in it.

5. HEEE as in the word HEAT. The EEE sound related to the head region (both brow and crown chakras) is the high potency vowel that gives a quick fix of energy, as in the sound HEAVE. You place this sound into the head region sending stimulating vibrations into the brain. To increase its effectiveness, men can use their falsetto voice, that is, the high-pitched sound of their former boy's voice.

These five have been chosen as being most common. Of course, in life we hear in spontaneous laughter mixtures or modifications of these. In fact, you may wonder why people laugh the way they do. It is quite possible that it is more than a personality trait, that the deep psyche knows which laugh suits their nature best for purposes of cleansing body, mind, and spirit. It can easily occur when the laughter exercises grow apace—the intended sound will revert to your natural laugh. Keep to that and return to the intended sound at the start of another cycle.

In producing these rhythmic laughter sounds, keep the mouth fairly wide open. Do not be tight-lipped about it. You want to be laughing uproariously at all times. You might even induce giggles or even a laughing fit where the laughter continues beyond your control. Actually, within limits, such giggles are a good sign, demonstrating that you have opened up a channel of joyous, free-flowing energy.

No one laughs without the body moving or shaking in some way. So while doing your induced rhythmic laughing, shake your body convulsively all over. Make your body entirely loose, even the head and neck region. This is a clear-cut letting-go ritual which demands no inhibitions on your part. The hands, in particular, will be used differently for each region and corresponding vowel sound.

1. HUH. Simply shake your hands near your groin region.
2. HOH. With palms towards the body, move your hands in wide circles near and around your belly as though you were rubbing it with glee.
3. HAH. In making it a hearty laugh, imagine your bioenergetic heart extending out from your physical heart. Hold that heart in the palms of your hands and play with that heart, bouncing it lightly up and down.
4. HEH. Uplift your head slightly while keeping the body in movement and place your hands a few inches from the throat area, slightly shaking them.
5. HEE. Place your hands above your head, palms down and make circular, whirling movements around the crown of your head.

Feel free to work with the laughter sounds. You might select only one or two on any given occasion rather than do all five. You might find that, through experience, some provide you with greater benefits than others. As far as duration is concerned, do no more than 3 minutes of laughing before taking at least a minute's rest. Overall, the whole process need not be longer than 20 minutes—2 minutes of laughing and 2 minutes' rest for each vowel sound change.

Groaning

Groaning is the fundamental natural sound to express frustration, being thwarted and, at its most intense, anger. It is an attempt to let off the pressure of some blockage within. Unlike swearing, which increases the negative emotion, groaning is the natural way to diffuse such feelings safely. The vowel sound that best expresses this is AW as in "Awe." Certainly we have all heard people spontaneously use the sound when they have been thwarted or something has gone wrong or their feelings are hurt. It is also heard in the American South in the form of the folksy "Aw shucks." This AW sound is represented in the emotional words *wrought, overwrought, distraught,* and even *awful.* It is very much about tightness within yourself, especially in the solar plexus region. In life this tightness can be expressed in a sense of duty without love, "I OUGHT (awt) to be doing this or that."

The practice of groaning can be applied to actual situations in which you release the emotions described safely. It is well recognized that the suppression of such emotions works negatively on the nervous system and causes blockages and rigidity in the energy flow. On the other hand, even if you do not find yourself in this state, you can benefit from groaning because there is always a certain amount of tension that builds up in the solar plexus region due to stress and worry. The object is to use the principle of resonance—that is, through the sound of AW—to shake loose the "OUGHTness" of any blockages there.

In order to build a fire in the belly, so to speak, the R consonant is placed in front of the AW vowel. The RR sound is the chief representative of the fire element among the consonants (see chapter 6). This consonant is used to stimulate the solar plexus region in both Tantra Yoga and Tibetan Buddhist traditions. To give the R its strongest resonance, it has to be sounded as ERRR as in the word "error." The combination produces the word RAW, as in "raw courage" and "raw emotion," where the vibrations of the solar plexus are freed to operate at their maximum. In this respect, you are to become like roaring lions. It is not a beautiful sound but rough-hewn, and the deeper the sound the better.

This can be achieved through keeping the jaw loose and the throat wide open. Stay on the ERRR sound for at least 5 seconds before sliding into the AW. Visualize yourself having a stomachache. Listen to your vowel sound, noting the shape of the mouth. Remember that AW is a nasal sound that gets into the nose. There can be a tendency for this vowel to drift into another variant of an A sound.

A Groaning Ritual

To act out this sound in movement, stand as usual, with your feet comfortably apart. Feel yourself sunk deeply into the floor, with knees slightly bent. Place your clenched fists, representing all the tensions, onto your abdominal region. As the ERRAW sound emerges, start bending the body forwards, keeping the fists in place. This gesture enacts regurgitation, getting rid of all those impurities within the solar plexus. Do

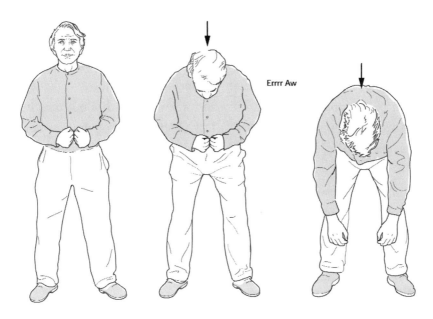

Errrr Aw

not bend any further than is comfortable. When your sound concludes, release the fists from the belly and let your arms hang loose. This basic hanging position corresponds to a state of catharsis. Stay down for at least 30 seconds before slowly rising up and bringing yourself to the original position. If you are really letting go with the full force of this sound, then ten cycles is more than enough to do the work. Conclude with the silent meditation.

Keening

The word *keening,* originating in Ireland, is another word for "wailing" as in the emotion of sorrow. It is a descending or ascending siren sound on the EE vowel—in other words, our high-frequency range. Note that the English words relating to sorrow—*grief, weep,* and *cry* (in lengthened form) and, of course, *keening*—all contain the EE sound. A good number of people contain within their psyche some kind of sorrow and/or regrets that they have allowed to color and so limit their true nature. However, keening can serve a wider purpose than alleviating sorrow and regrets. The EE sound, as our highest-frequency vowel, offers us a quick energy fix, not least because there are a far greater number of cells in the brain that respond to the upper range of frequencies.[5] At the same time, the siren sound of EEE passes through a great multiple of frequencies, enabling our bodies to choose which ones they are in sympathetic vibration with for sound health. Both the physical and bioenergetic bodies can select on the basis of the resonance principle.

To increase the effectiveness of this cleansing and energizing soundwork, the sound of K can precede the EEE so that you are actually intoning the very sound of keening. In terms of high-potency energy, it relates directly to the emotion of enthusiasm as expressed in the adjective "keen" (see chapter 6). This K (or the hard C sound) serves a similar purpose as the H sound in the laughter work, that is, to stimulate the glandular system. Whereas the energy of the H sound rushed upward from the abdomen impacting into the upper regions of the head, the K sound does the reverse. Its sharp, cutting sound, as in an arrow hitting a target, strikes the back of the neck and then speeds downward along the spine, sending off its energies to those glands along the way. The Mayans of Central America connect the K sound with solar energy in their seed-syllable chant K'IN (see chapter 10).

First practice making the biting sound of K, thinking of the word "cut." Only produce the pure K without adding any vowel sounds such as "Ka." Experience how the throat locks at the outset of making the K sound. Do this several times without exploding the K. Then practice allowing the K to explode, thinking of the word "cut." After the explosive K let all the air continue to escape, squeezing the abdominal muscles powerfully and effectively.

In the ritual you will need two breaths. First, one for the K and then another deep one for the EEE. It is quite a simple process. Let your voice begin on any high note and then slowly slide it downwards like a siren. Men have the choice of working with their falsetto voice (as suggested in the laughter sound of HEE-HEEE) or staying within the confines of their natural voice. The falsetto voice is the preferred method because of the higher frequencies involved. As the man's voice descends, it can change over to the natural voice if there is sufficient breath. It is important that the mouth be wide and the throat open so that the EEE sound is bright. It is not to be a sound of fright where the throat feels constricted. This might hurt the voice. The conclusion of the siren is when you have exhausted your breath. Or the siren sound could be moved slightly down and up within the overall descent, using more than one breath. Project the sound like a cry for help. Better to have an intensity than a long duration of the siren.

A Keening Ritual

To encourage the voice in this process, join it to this movement.

1. Place your right foot in front of your left, the right foot pointing forward and the left pointing straight-left, as in a fencing position. The weight of your body is on the forward foot.

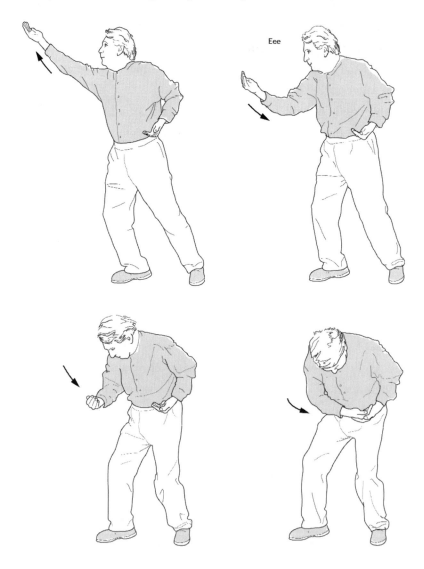

2. Lift up your right arm, palm upward, hand slightly cupped as though you wish to receive something from above. Place your left hand, palm up, alongside your body at waist level. As you make the descending siren sound, move your right hand in a straight line down toward your left, looking deeply into the right at all times. In doing this, bend the upper body forward as in bowing and slowly bend the knees, allowing the weight of the body to shift to the back foot. This is akin to a gesture of sorrow.

3. At the conclusion, the right hand, still palm up, comes to rest in the palm of the left hand. The speed of the movement of the right into the left is based upon the length of your breath. The hands should meet at the point where your breath has run out. So as you draw down the sound you have to pay attention to how long your breath is.

4. Once in the bowed position, remain there for at least 30 seconds, breathing normally. Then, slowly go in reverse to the original position, maintaining eye contact with the rising right hand. Do this for a maximum of nine cycles.

As a kind of by-product of keening, the siren sound of EEE can also be used as a form of vocal scanning. The process begins the same as keening. As the EEE sound descends you carefully monitor its relationship to your body, attempting to ascertain if there is any place along route where the sound has a particular resonating effect, as though it is opening a channel for healing. If such points are found, keep the voice at that frequency, taking breath as needed to continue that vibration. Depending on where you feel this point in yourself, feel free to change the vowel sound accordingly (see chapter 11). To encourage the steady flow of the sliding vibrations, stand or sit in a comfortable position and place your hands above and in front of your head, fingers pointing upward and palms facing inward. As you draw down the siren sound, likewise draw down the hands, slowly past your face and all the way down to the groin. As you reach the heart your fingers will naturally point towards each other. This is a good exercise in developing your intuition in sensing where in the body particular frequencies have strong and positive effects.

Sighing

When people have anxious, fearful, or even threatening moments in their lives which then pass away without harm, they often breathe a sigh of relief. They throw off the tensions built up at those times. The vowel sound usually produced is either OH or OO, depending on the intensity of these emotions, OH being the greater of the two. What the body/mind mechanism desires is to SOOTHE the nervous system which has gone out of balance. The OO vowel corresponds to the element of water which has a great capacity to relax our bodies. Many people take to lying in a bath or taking a shower or swimming to relieve tension in their muscular system. So the purpose of sighing as a therapeutic natural sound is to blow off general stress that tightens the nervous system and then lodges in the muscles, and consequently to bring about calm and deep peace.

A Sighing Ritual

1. To achieve the sound, assume the usual standing position and draw in a deep breath. Simultaneously, uplift your arms over your head so that the arms are rounded, the wrists relaxed, and the fingers pointed downward over the head.

2. Begin with an SSS sound, allotting it about 2 to 3 seconds. Imagine its sound emerging out of the center of your forehead, the seat of the so-called "third eye." Directly follow with OO (as in "soothe"), beginning on a relatively high-

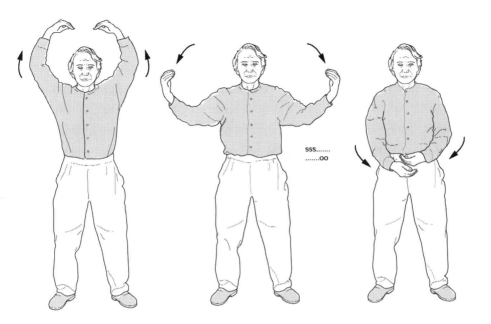

sss.......
........oo

pitched tone that does not constrict your throat. Let the
downward slides eventually lead you to your deepest tone
until the sound disappears. Make the sound slightly breathy
in character, just as you would hear a sigh when it occurs
spontaneously. At the same time, lower your arms sideways
in a circle so that they fall in front of your body at the level
of your groin. In circular fashion and in silence, lift up your
arms once again while taking in the next breath.

3. Return to the original position and start again. Do as many
cycles as you feel necessary. Conclude with a silent period of
at least 3 minutes during which you follow your breathing.

Humming

In certain Eastern forms of meditation the sound of MMM closes such sacred seed syllables as OM, HUM, HAM, and RAM, and in the West it forms an integral part of AMEN. It is the agent that helps to draw us into a profound state of quietude, relaxation, and peace. Its comforting sound leads us deep within where we can find our true sense of self and therefore have great realizations and original ideas. In this respect it has a strong link with the brow chakra, the seat of insight. It is no accident that we emit a kind of humming sound when we make a discovery, when something is revealed to us or understood, or when we are in agreement or in tune with another person's thoughts. The humming MMM is a life-affirming sound, one that almost universally mothers use to still their children as in a lullaby or adults produce in a state of contentment.[6]

The MMM consonant has a rich buzzing noise like a bumble bee that can bring great balance to our emotions, diminishing our egotistical side by slowing down the lesser, moving mind, and tapping into the higher mind. It can also shake loose in a safe and happy manner emotions that need releasing. Is it any wonder that the sound of a BEE relates to our BEING? As an alternative to Shakespeare's "To be or not to be," we might substitute the phrase, "To hum or not to hum," as applied to sound therapy.

A Humming Ritual

To allow the natural sound of MMM to do its best work, draw in a slow, deep breath and try different tones from high to low to see which one resonates your head region most vibrantly. Essentially the MMM is a nasalization of vocal sound. This can be shown by pinching your nose and hearing how the sound shuts down. The object is to vibrate the MMM first in the head region and then allow it to seep down into the upper chest. Make the sound strong, buzzy, and bright by putting a smile on your face. To hear the sound in its full resonance, place the index fingers lightly over your ears with the rest of your hand embracing your face. This ritual can be done either sitting down or standing up. Have gaps between the hummings where you will breathe normally and observe what happens. Then take in another slow, deep breath just before emitting the next pro-longed MMM sounding. And so on. It would not be surprising if you felt like falling asleep. This would be a good sign of equa-nimity within yourself and would show that you have slowed down the physical and mental processes while balancing and purifying the emotions.

At the conclusion of toning any of these natural sounds, allow for a period of silence, leaving its duration to your natural sense. There are different approaches to being in this silence and these are outlined in chapter 4.

9

Discovering Your Fundamental Tone

If each human being is a unique multitude of frequency vibration patterns at all levels, then it follows that there is one fundamental tone which is at the root of their existence, a tone that represents the pure essence of that person, that is synonymous with their soul. Vocalizing that tone would send sympathetic vibrations to the root, awakening the fine energy that assists in their spiritual unfoldment. It is a vibrational point of reference that can be sounded at any time, even hummed as you walk along, for example. It is also practical to have such a tone when toning or chanting on a single frequency. So, in the case of toning OM alone, you can choose to use your fundamental tone rather than selecting a tone arbitrarily.

The process of finding this tone in yourself requires patience and perseverance as it is carried out over a period of at least two weeks on a daily basis. The prerequisite is that you have a method for placing yourself into a deeply relaxed state. This could be either meditation, yoga, deep-breathing exercises, or working with therapeutic vocal sound. In this manner you are enabled to get in touch with a tone that is a reflection of your essential self.

Another necessity is to have some sort of instrument to determine what tones you are producing. As mentioned in chapter 7, it is very helpful to have a small electronic keyboard which contains all possible tones. Being portable, it can be placed quite near you for easy access. It is better than a piano because there are organ-like sounds on the keyboard that will remain sustained as long as your finger depresses the key. This is a distinct advantage when searching for tones. The tuning forks that are currently available give only the white notes of the keyboard, missing out the many semitones offered by the black keys. A pitch pipe has all the tones but is awkward to use. Alternatively, a cassette player could be used. Record the tone produced each day and then compare them at the end of the experiment. This method requires a certain degree of tonal memory for the comparison between all the notes recorded.

The next step in the process is to lie down in a very comfortable position. It is your choice to have the head supported by a pillow or the knees raised. To be more in touch with the resonance of the tone you will produce within the body, place one hand over the chest region, the other over the solar plexus region. This touch might help to confirm what tones are the most in tune with your essence. Have the keyboard or tape recorder as well as some paper and a pen ready. Set the keyboard on a quiet flute sound so that it will not overwhelm your voice.

Next draw in a deep breath (explained in chapter 5) through your mouth which is to be shaped to form the vowel OO (as in "food"). On the outbreath, through the small aperture of the lips, it is important that you allow a tone to ooze out from deep within you so that you feel you are merely an instrument being played upon. It is likely, therefore, that there will be no sound at all during the first few outbreaths. Only a soft rush of air. This can be for as long as 2 minutes. It is important to take your time. Gradually your vocal cords will find a certain tension that produces an actual tone. Let it emerge quietly. Once it is established, you can allow it to get louder. Do not allow it to deviate.

If a tape recorder is used, there is nothing to do except let the tone be well-recorded. If a keyboard is your source, then you will have to sit up while sustaining your tone. Assuming you do not have perfect pitch,* depress the middle C key (women) or the C one octave below (men). This is a critical moment because (a) you must not let the keyboard notes you play in passing influence the maintenance of your own note and (b) you have to determine whether your tone is higher (to the right) or lower (to the left) than that C, a basic musical skill which most people have naturally. Move your finger along note by note, including the black keys, until your ears tell you that you have reached a matching tone. There is the possibility that your tone will lie between two keyboard notes, in the crack so to speak. The choice will have to be made whether to go with the higher or lower tone. Then write down the name of your note (see chapter 7 explaining the set-up of a piano keyboard). More than likely, your tone will not be higher than the G above the C nor lower than the F below the C played.

There is an alternative to this method. It is a kind of vocal scanning. Start with the outlined preparations. Then, instead of sounding a singular tone, initiate any tone on the OO vowel and then slide your voice up and down in siren fashion. You are attempting to find a strong resonance point in yourself where you feel your body in vibratory synchronization with the sound you are producing. The sliding must be done slowly in order to cover and hear as many frequencies as possible. When found, hold on to it and then record it either using a keyboard or the cassette player as indicated above.

Continue this process for two weeks or longer until there is sufficient recurrence of a particular tone for you to come to the conclusion that you have fixed on it. It should have a certain tingling sensation in the whole of your body that makes you feel happy.

---

* The ability to know what note you are producing without reference to any instrument.

GROUP NAME CHANTING

A great mystery surrounds the origins of all languages, the greatest question being, "Was there a single root language in pre-history from which all others are descended?" Equal to this question is, "Is there a direct correlation between the names of objects and actions and the objects and actions themselves?" To a certain extent this has its realization in Genesis when Adam names all the animals, birds, and beasts. Does the object known as a "tree" contain vibrations that resonate with the sound of the word *tree*? Taking this idea to its ultimate, could the prolonged group chanting of the sound "tree" cause a tree to grow healthier roots, produce more fruit, or be protected from disease? Such an idea is built upon the premise that there are no accidents in the unfoldment of life. All has a meaning and a purpose.

If you have a sense that this is so, then it follows that the name given to you at birth also has a meaning and purpose. How could it be otherwise? In fact, the letters of NAME are an anagram for AMEN, a sound descended from OM and essentially a mantra in the Christian tradition meaning "so be it," that is, surrendering to the highest source. Perhaps you were aware of this name to be given to you even before your birth or you heard it being proposed while still in the womb. Even if your parents do not choose your name in some intuitive way—for example, naming you after one of your grandparents—it does not mean that the name is without meaning and purpose. For a start, we know that many traditional names have a meaning. But what is their purpose as a vibration when sounded out? Do they conform in some way to your own network of frequencies? Have you felt that your name never conformed to who you are and gone to the length of changing it? Have you modified your name? As your nature has changed, have you thought that you have outgrown your name? Whatever the case, it is proposed that the chanting of your name by a group in your presence positively feeds your essence and brings you into loving unity with those who do the chanting. At the same time you become so much more sensitive to the consonants and vowels operating within your name/sound. You stop experiencing it as a name and it becomes totally a vibration.

Name Chanting Ritual

Form a circle of chanters who either stand or sit in chairs or on the floor. The person whose name is to be chanted sits or lies down in the center of the circle. If lying down it is best if the circle of chanters is sitting on the floor. Everyone closes their eyes so that their hearing will be uppermost. Ask the person receiving in what form they want their name chanted.

If the person whose name is to be chanted has discovered a fundamental tone, it makes sense to use it. Otherwise, let that person find a tone spontaneously prior to the chanting and then have all the chanters use that. It gives the ritual a more personal touch. The chanting can be either slow or fast. In the slow form, each syllable of the name is stretched out, the last elongated to about double the length. Have a brief pause between each sounding. It is very helpful at the beginning if someone in the circle leads like a conductor, indicating the start and the changes from one syllable to another until the group feels the different lengths with each successive repetition. Then the eyes can be closed. This is especially important for names ending in clear-cut consonants so that the group chants them together. These should be done crisply. In the fast form, each syllable is about 1 to 2 seconds in length and the repeated sounding of the name is continuous without break. Breath is taken as needed. Or you can begin in the slow mode so that the person really has a deeper taste of his or her name and then switch to the fast steady-state mode. Use your discretion about the duration. At least 2 minutes of chanting would be good.

10

Mantras, Chanting, and Vocal Improvisation

There are three essential interrelated approaches to using vocal sound therapeutically. Toning, which has already been presented in relation to natural sounds (chapter 8) and the use of mantras and chanting. In all cases their primary feature is repetition, allowing the chosen sounds to penetrate deeply into the psyche and from there into the areas where they will be of most benefit. This could be in relation to stilling the mind, raising the general energy level, or releasing a blockage. In ordinary parlance, to chant is to repeat a spoken or musical phrase. In this sense a mantra is chanted and even toning might be considered by some as a form of chanting. The following are definitions that give some differentiation between them:

♪ TONING: This is the repetition of single sounds or syllables. The vowels are the essence of these sounds and are usually stretched out longer than normal speech. They can be preceded and/or succeeded by consonant sounds as is the case in toning the chakras (see chapter 11). The toning can be directed not only to specific areas of the body but also to the emotional body as was shown with the natural sounds (chapter 8).

♪ MANTRAS: These are often referred to as sacred sounds because they are part of the practice of different religious traditions. *Mantra* is a Sanskrit word whose literal meaning is "that which protects and purifies the mind." Here *mind* represents not only thought but also feelings. These sounds, each of which is a kind of germinating seed (in Sanskrit *bija*) that is implanted in the mind, are catalysts for ridding ourselves of traits that impede our spiritual unfoldment. Like toning and chanting they are sounded repetitively in a steady rhythm. They can be sounded either inwardly or aloud. Done inwardly within the mind, no tone is needed. Only the rhythm is necessary. This inner repetition is useful because it can be set in motion at any time and in any situation.

♪ CHANTING: This is actually a form of singing characterized by the repetition of short phrases of tones, fairly narrow in range, often wedded to some kind of sacred text and done as part of a ritual. A good example of a body of chants are those of the North American Indians.

MANTRAS

The chief purpose of sounding out mantras is to expand and elevate our state of consciousness. That is, to get rid of negative tendencies embedded in the psychology and consequently to put us in touch with our real self. As our emotions are purified in the process, not only will there be a sharp clarity of mind but also the physical body will enter deep states of relaxation enabling it to heal itself. This is about coming into wholeness.

The following are a selection of often-used mantras which have been categorized according to religious traditions.* Most can be done on a single tone, a few are like melodies but narrow in range, and one is sounded solely on the breath. Each has a commentary about the meaning of the sounds and how they are to be executed.

The length of time for intoning any of these mantras lies with your judgment. A recommended duration is 5 to 10 minutes. A good practice is to produce them at a medium to loud volume. As you draw to a close, diminish the volume and let the sound move within your consciousness. Feel your vocal cords still shaping the sound until it is transformed into some kind of rhythm of its own accord and reaches as silent a state as possible. The inner silence can last easily for 10 to 20 minutes. For further guidance, see the "Silence and Meditation" section of chapter 4.

Hinduism and Tibetan Buddhism

OM AUM RAUM

These are the supreme mantras as they represent the great echo of the original divine Word or Logos. For the Hindus this sound is also equated with the universe beyond form. In the openness and circularity of the OH sound you can sense all the possibilities realized and unrealized in yourself—the many. Thus, this sound is directly related to the Latin word *omnes* which translates as "everything or all." On the other side of the globe, the Mayans also recognize the OM sound, linking O with the heavens and higher consciousness and the M with the Earth. With each MMM sounding the lips close to a small rounded point—out of the many come individual points of creation. The Hindus believe similarly that this combination of sounds symbolizes the beginning and end of creation. This is represented in the ancient Greek phrase *Alpha* and *OMega*, the first and the last. The balancing of the OH and MMM enables us to have a clarity and stillness of being and so be attuned to

---

* A set of mantric chants worthy of exploration and not included here are those channeled by Frank Alper and known as the Atlantean chants. See resources.

our true thoughts, feelings, and the creativity beyond the ego. When we are bathed in the aura of this mantra we can have glimpses of who we really are.

To chant the OM sound is to direct it from the head and move it downward through the body into the belly. This naturally expands its energy field. This drawing down of the sound into the belly is enhanced by preceding the OH vowel with the AH, representing the heart and its attributes of wonder, adoration, and love. The twofold vowel sound corresponds to the Sanskrit spelling of AUM. In fact, the Hindus consider AH to be one of four primary mantric syllables, the others being OM, HUM, and HRIH. The AH requires you to begin with an even wider mouth. To give the mantra further vibratory power, place the fire element of ERR before either the OH or AH-OO combination. Ensure that you feel the mantra vibrating as much of the body as possible. In part, this is achieved through the elongation of each vowel and consonant. Especially lengthen the final M. Whichever form is used, equally divide each aspect of the sound over a period of 10–15 seconds. Alternatively, any of these can be pulsed rhythmically so that each repetition lasts around 2 seconds or a bit slower. Either the slow or fast version will induce a fine state of meditation.

Normally the mantra is repeated on a single tone. If you have found a satisfying fundamental tone, use it. Otherwise, find a tone that is not too high and provides you with a solid resonance. For the musically knowledgeable, select from these tones according to vocal ranges: Basses: G up to D. Tenors: C up to G. Altos: A up to E. Sopranos: C up to G. For group work, the middle C for women and the octave below for men suits well. These instructions apply to all the succeeding mantras chanted on a single tone.

If the sounding of the OM is done standing up, the following movements can be added as a visualization.

A Ritual for Intoning OM

Balance yourself by standing with your feet positioned under your shoulders. Relax the knees. Cup both your hands, placing the right hand over the left, the left palm facing up. It is as though you are holding a tennis ball. Situate the hands in front of the solar plexus region. Visualize the inside of the hands as a ball of energy emerging from the solar plexus. As you intone the OM allow the hands to part slowly as though the round shape of the ball is ever increasing. How far the expansion of the ball extends is your choice. During its growth you can move your hands as you wish as long as they are opposite each other. They could be at any angle. Be playful with the ball. When nearing completion, return the hands to the original position.

OM SHANTI (OHMMM SHAHN-TEE)

Translation: May you live in the peace of the Universal sound.

In the illustration below, each syllable of this extended OM mantra is given a duration; in musical terms, a number of beats. A simple way of working is to set the beat rate to 1 beat per second and follow a clock or wrist watch to start. This is a relatively slow speed. Once the steadiness is established, you could increase the tempo to your own liking. It is also given in musical rhythm notation for those who can read it. This approach applies to all the succeeding mantras which are assigned beat patterns.

OM	SHAN	TI
2	1	3
𝅗𝅥	𝅘𝅥	𝅗𝅥.

This beat pattern corresponds to the natural flow of the three sounds as you might pronounce them slowly in natural speech and is used when continuously repeating the mantra. In this case you have to catch your breath as you can. Otherwise, pause at the end of each sounding, prolonging the final TEE and fully replenishing your breath. The movement expanding the ball of energy described above can also be joined to this mantra.

SOHAM (SO-HAHMMM)

Translation: I am That.

According to both Hindu and Buddhist traditions, this meditative mantra on the breath is considered to be the vibration of the cosmic unheard AUM and produces a union between the individual and the universal consciousness. The two seed syllables are the polarity of female Yin energy, represented by SO, and male Yang energy, represented by HAM. There are three further polarities inherent in SOHAM: inspiration (SO—cold air) and expiration (HAM—warm air), mental (SO) and emotional (HAM) energies, and spirit (SO) and matter (HAM).

The mantra can be sounded inwardly and in time with the breath, SO with the inspiration and HAM with the expiration. It can also be resonated aloud. Producing the SO on the inbreath requires some skill and concentration as we are not accustomed to creating sound in this manner. It is not unlike that sudden intake of air with an intense, whispered OH when you are taken by surprise or realize that something has gone wrong. Begin by ensuring that you have an open throat by imagining that you are gargling. Draw in breath through the mouth, lips slightly apart, allowing the air as it passes the teeth to create a very short hissing SSS sound with a little help from the tongue. As the air rushes into the open-throat region, create a whispering OH sound. If done well it sounds like the wind through the trees. On the outbreath you form the whispering sound of HAH, gradually closing your lips to form a silent MMM. Ideally, the rhythm of the two sounds on the breath is even, each syllable being of the same duration.

Feel it as long, even pulsations like the perfect swing of a pendulum.

To bring the whole body into play with the mantra, add the following T'ai Chi-like movements.

Ritual Movements for Intoning SO-HAM

Stand with feet shoulder-width apart, knees bent. Extend your arms fully forward with palms facing upward, fingers together as in a slight cup. On the SO sound draw your hands toward your face. Move the palms of your hands to the face, imagining that the sound is entering your brow chakra. Then pass your hands downward over your face as though you were pouring cleansing water over it. During the downward movement visualize the SO descending all the way to the root chakra. As the hands move near the heart, turn the palms outward. At the heart, change to the HAM, feeling the sound being drawn up

SO

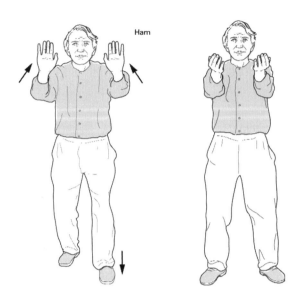

Ham

from the root and pushing the hands out very slowly as though moving a wall. At the same time take a small step forwards with either foot. Reach the silent M when the arms are fully extended. Immediately turn the palms upward and begin the next cycle with SO. The foot brought forward is returned to its original place as you draw the hands toward the face. Ideally, the flow of the movements should be continuous, in time with the rhythm of SO-HAM. At no point do the hand/arm movements stop. It is also possible to sit in a chair and do only the hand/arm gestures without moving the foot.

Do no more than eighteen cycles of actual sound. If using the movement, you can continue it for about nine cycles while silently sounding the mantra within. This is a very good way to draw it to a close. Thereafter sit down, inwardly following the slow rhythm of the SO-HAM and going into deep meditation. This applies also to those who omit the movements.

OM AH HUM

Translation: Enter into me, O Universal sound of OM.

This well-known mantra is found as part of more extended chants but is also done on its own. As a threefold mantra it represents the three aspects of the unfolding creative cycle: Creation itself (birth), Maintenance (the life process), and Dissolution (dying away). The three seed syllables can be sounded on a single tone or with a change of tone on the AH.

Whether using your own tone or the version above, keep to a seven-beat pulse: three for OM, one for AH and three for HUM. This means each time a quick breath has to be drawn in just before repeating the sequence without losing the beat. It is effective to use a slightly sliding sound as you move between notes. Do it sitting down in a good back-supporting chair. The following finger movements can be added.

Finger Movements for OM AH HUM Mantra

Rest your hands, palms up, on your thighs. In time to a medium to slow beat that you establish, touch with the right thumb the tips of the fifth, fourth, third, and second fingers of your right hand successively. Do the same with the left thumb and hand, leaving out the second finger. This provides the seven-beat structure.

NOTE: For the sake of simplicity, the presentation of mantras and chants in musical notation is set out using only the white notes of the piano keyboard. This is not necessarily the best range for all voices. Assuming that you can read musical notation, play through the notes to get the tune, so to speak. If it feels too high or too low, transpose it in your mind to where it resonates best for your voice.

OM MANI PADME HUM (OM MAH-NEE PAHD-MAY HOOM)

Translation: Hail, the jewel in the lotus.

This is the supreme mantra for Buddhists. *Mani*, the jewel, is the Divine that dwells in the heart, referred to as *padme*, the lotus. As always, the opening OM addresses the Absolute or Creator being, synonymous with the universal sound. The *hum* represents our individual self, a finite spark of the universal consciousness.

Sit in a back-supporting chair with your hands, palms up, on the thighs. Use either a single tone of your choice or the chant outlined below. Keep to a nine-beat cycle as follows:

Syllables	OM	MA	NI	PAD	ME	HUM	Breath
Beats	2	1	1	1	1	3	1

As musical chant:

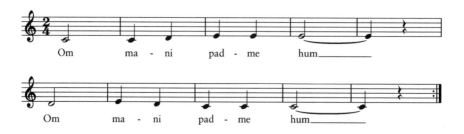

Islamic

ALLAH HU

These are two sacred sounds, each of which is a name for the supreme being. In chapter 6 it was noted that the AH sound is often part of the sound that people of many religions use in referring to the Godhead and that the L consonant, according to the Mayans, is the essence of vibration. Thus, in Allah there is a powerful simplicity in joining the two sounds. It is important, therefore, that the L sound be made particularly prominent by toning two distinct syllables, AL and LAH. On the AL the tongue rises up, the tip touching the upper palette just in front of the teeth. On the LAH the tongue is released down, resting in the bottom of the mouth.

It can be sounded with the spoken voice, with an intense whispered breath, or on any tone of your choice. Take pauses as necessary and briefly listen to the chant within. Then re-sound it aloud. According to the rhythm given, the AL is one beat and the LAH two, with the LAH receiving a slight accent. As you near the end, let the chanting grow softer and softer, turning it completely into a breath sound until it disappears within you. Then listen to its sound mentally as the entrance into meditative silence.

A typical rhythm for chanting ALLAH is in a three-beat pattern with the accent on the LAH. As follows:

Syllables	AL	LAH	AL	LAH	AL	LAH	etc.
Beats	1	2	1	2	1	2	

The sacred sound HUU can be joined to the ALLAH by sustaining it after a series of ALLAHs. For example, chant ALLAH four times. After one beat of silence (breath), sound the HUU on a slightly higher tone than the ALLAH or a tone of your choice if the ALLAH is done on a breath sound. Then take a one-beat breath and continue these cycles.

As always keep to a moderate amount of duration, using pauses as necessary. Towards the end discontinue the HUU and follow the previous instructions, allowing the volume to fade and the rhythm of the ALLAH to sink into your mental sphere as a mantra for meditation.

There are many ALLAH HUU chants in the Sufi tradition. Instead of sounding the HUU on a singular note, it can be sung on a series of notes, for example. Here is one such example:

Huu

If these sacred sounds are chanted in a group, participants should gather in a circle with their arms around each other's waists. As they intone the ALLAH or ALLAH HUU (following the guidelines given above), they sway the circle to the left and then to the right. The swaying left occurs on the first LAH, the swaying right on the second, and from there on alternating. This fits in with an essentially three-beat pattern which is continued during the sounding of the HUU, if added to the ALLAHs. Once again, allow the chanting to decrease in volume until there is no outward sound. Continue the swaying movement while repeating the sound within. Finally, have a stillness of the movement and a comparable stillness of mind.

Christian

ALLELUIA (AHL-LAY-LOO-YAH)

Translation (from the Hebrew Halleluyah, Praise ye Yahweh): Praise ye the Lord.

This four-syllable mantra is comparable to the ALLAH in its repeated use of the highly vibratory sound of L. Its threefold vowel sequence directs itself to the heart (AH), throat (AY), and belly (OO) regions.

Moreover, the Y sound, as it links with Yahweh—a name of God also rendered as Jehovah—is central to the toning of the heart in the great Tantra Yoga tradition.

As with ALLAH, allow the tip of the tongue to reach up to the upper palette in front of the teeth on AL and LU. Chant it on a tone of your choice, or fundamental tone, in this nine-beat pattern (including breath) with a slight accent on the LU. Alternatively, change to a note two steps down (as in Sol–Mi) for the final YAH. Diminish its volume gradually and allow it to become an inner mantra. As follows:

Syllables	AHL	LAY	LOO	YAH	Breath
Beats	1	1	3	3	1

KYRIE ELEISON (KEAR-REE-AY AY-LAY-EE-SOHN)

Translation (from the Greek): Lord, have mercy.

This Christian mantra, which is a very direct prayer, has a potent set of upper-range vowels affecting the head (the EE three times) and the throat (the AY three times). At the same time its consonants resonate four primary centers—the K which starts at the back of the neck and sends an awakening vibration down the spine, the S that focuses itself at the brow, the R that is centered in the solar plexus, and the L that stimulates the base of the spine.

Sound the mantra on the tone of your choice or fundamental tone. Alternatively, change to a note two steps lower (as in Sol–Mi) for the final SON. Give an impetus to each cycle by accentuating the opening K. Take quick breaths just after closing on the N. The twelve-beat pattern, which for Christians could symbolize the twelve apostles, can be mirrored in gesture by touching the tips of the fingers, the fifth through the second, three times with the thumb in the same manner as described for OM AH HUM. This can be done with either the left or right hand.

After a time, allow its sound to diminish and find its way within, acting as a catalyst for meditation.

Syllables	KY	RI	E	E	LE	I	SON	Breath
Beats	1	1	3	1	1	1	3	1

Alternatively, the Kyrie Eleison can be sung on a series of notes as a repeated chant. Here is one such example.

Ky - ri - e   E - - - le - i son___

MARANATHA (MAH-RAH-NAH-THAH)

Translation (from the Aramaic): Come, Lord *or* the Lord comes.

This four-syllable word appears at the end of Corinthians I (16:22) in the New Testament and has been adopted as a mantra by the Christian Meditation Movement founded by the Catholic Benedictine monk John Main in the 1980s.[1] With its series of AH vowels it is a mantra totally centered in the heart. Choose a comfortable tone, or your fundamental, for its outward projection. Make each sound of equal duration at an easy-going pace and, if you like, use the finger movements described above with either the left or right hand. Take breaths as required as the mantra is repeated continuously. Use your intuition to change over into an inner sounding, feeling ever so slightly the movements of the vocal cords.

Syllables	MA	RA	NA	THA
Beats	1	1	1	1

Mayan

K'IN (KK-EEN)*

This is the Mayan mantra sound that connects with the sun and its life-giving energy. The prayer that accompanies it is: "Father Sun, give me strength / Father Sun, make me wise / Father Sun, make me into a seed / Father Sun, make me eternal." In the ritual the chanters stand facing in the direction of the sun with their arms out to the sides, elbows bent at 90 degrees so that the palms of the hands are at the level of the head and facing forward. Before starting, it is required to blow out a long silent breath from the mouth. As with keening (chapter 8), the opening K is sounded sharply so as to strike the back of the neck. There follows a very tiny gap of silence before sounding the EEN, holding it for the full length of the breath. It is best done as a group ritual. After striking the K, group members each produce spontaneously their own tone on the EEN or a predetermined singular tone. Do the chanting in sets of seven, renewing the breath after each one, and then take a minute's pause. Three sets are quite enough to experience deeply the mantra's power.

SINGING CHANTS

In addition to the examples of singing chants presented earlier for Allah Huu and Kyrie Eleison, here are four more that I have used in my workshops. Although there is no reason for not chanting them by yourself, their vibrations carry more benefit when done collectively.

Hindu

SRI RAM (SHREE RAHM)

Translation: Honor and victory to Rama.

In India, the chanting of a mantra in the form of singing is called a *bhajan*. Often they are devotional in nature and are then referred to as

---

* As given by Hunbatz Men, an authority on Mayan civilization. See recommended reading.

kirtana. Their vibrations are most inspiring when sung with a group. The basic translation of the two versions of "Sri Ram" is "Honor and Victory to Rama." The second version adds the universal OM. Even though this is homage to a Hindu deity, it has a power far beyond its religious context due to the interplay of the broad vowels and consonants. It will act as a catalyst for deep silence as the chanters allow it gradually to seep into their inner consciousness.

A phonetic form of the text is given in parentheses for pronunciation.

Sri	Ram	Jay	Ram	Ja-	Ya	Ja-	Ya	Ram
(Shree)	(Rahm)	(Jay)	(Rahm)	(Jai)	(Yah)	(Jai)	(Yah)	(Rahm)

Someone in the group has to find a silent way of bringing the chant to an end before it continues on within. This could be done by sounding bells indicating that there will be three more repetitions of the chant. In this way people's eyes can remain closed.

Native American

The Indian tribes of North America offer quite an array of singing chants. Many are celebratory, extolling the wonders in their life. As with all chants of great spiritual traditions, they can open the heart and still the mind of anyone who surrenders to their power. At the deepest level, the participant and the chant become one and there is the feeling that you are being chanted. The addition of drums and rattle-type instruments is effective. The group should stand or sit in a circle. If instruments are not used, the group can join hands, linking up the circle to represent wholeness. To draw it to a close, a group member stationed at the center of the circle could give a hand signal indicating how many more repetitions remain or use bell sounds so eyes can stay shut, if desired.

WOA YEA

(Arapaho chant depicting wolves' mating calls)

HEY YUNGUA

(Chippewa welcoming song)

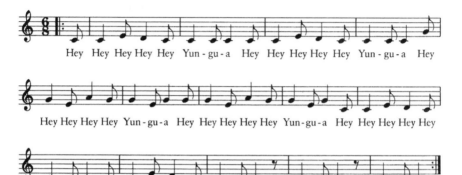

COLLECTIVE IMPROVISED SINGING

When working with therapeutic vocal sound in groups it is beneficial for group members to express their own sounds as a collective. This is best done after the group has worked a certain amount with natural sounds, toning, and chanting. The energy released from the previous soundwork enables the chanters in such rituals to experience an expressive freedom with their voices that they would normally find difficult to achieve.

The group can place restrictions on the improvisation, such as limiting it to one vowel and not using any consonants, or they can leave it wide open with vowel changes and the inclusion of consonants. Members stand closely in a circle so that they can put their arms around each other's waist as suggested in the chanting of Allah Huu. This arrangement provides a basis for the energy generated to pass right around the circle. In order to begin the ritual spontaneously, one individual should count to three, and as soon as the three is heard the whole group immediately starts up their vocalizing. Each member of the group must listen intently to the sounds of the whole so that there is some sort of integration of the vocal lines. This is about wholeness, not individuality.

Once started, the improvised singing is free to develop as it wants. Often it gradually grows dynamically, subsides for a time, and then builds up to a new crest and so on. Or it might remain meditative, keeping to soft sounds. This is the special magic of this ritual. It is a great opportunity for people to really experience a profound unity with each other where all personality barriers disappear and a single blissful organism is established.

There are two choices for ending the improvisation. The best situation is that all the members realize intuitively that they have come to the end and the sounds just fade away. The alternative is for one person to withdraw from the circle after a period of about 10 minutes. They will then decide on an appropriate point to draw to a close and ring some kind of gentle bell (a pair of small Tibetan cymbals, for example) to do so. It should be at a point where there is a natural subsidence of sound. The group remains standing in silence until the bells are rung again, bringing the proceedings to a close.

It is well worth recording these collective improvisations because they are more often than not beautiful pieces of contemporary music with a transcendent quality that many present-day composers do not achieve in their premeditated work. At the same time, the participants gain the satisfaction of hearing to what extent they have reached a deeper level in themselves where intuition and true freedom reign.

11

Toning the Chakras

The word *chakra* translates from the Sanskrit as "wheel." Chakras are vortices of whirling energy located between the base of the spine and the crown of the head. They are the receptors, mediators, and distributors within the body of subtle energy that is our auric or bioenergetic field. It is this surrounding aura that vitalizes the atoms of the physical body.

The subtle energy field consists of three channels—known in India as *nadis*—that relate to our cerebro-spinal and sympathetic nervous systems. Along the central channel that runs beside the spine lie seven principal chakras. These in turn are linked to and regulate the system of endrocrine glands, a vital part of the anatomy in maintaining good health. These glands are also intertwined with our emotions; negative states of mind will cause disturbances in their function. Equally, they govern all aspects of our physical constitution[1] and are associated with certain psychological qualities, the senses, and the elements. Thus, if there are particular physical ailments or negative states of mind that require healing vibrations, these correspondences can assist in choosing which seed mantras are most beneficial.

TABLE OF CORRESPONDENCES

Chakra and Position	Gland	Element	Sense	Quality	Physical Aspect Governed	Mental Disturbances
ROOT Between anus and genitals	Adrenals	Earth	Smell	Security	Spinal column, Kidneys	Insecurity
SACRAL 1–2" below navel	Gonads	Water	Taste	Sexuality, Creativity	Reproductive system	Powerlessness
SOLAR PLEXUS Between sternum and navel	Pancreas	Fire	Sight	Willpower	Stomach, Liver, Gall bladder, Nervous system	Fear
HEART Next to physical heart, at center	Thymus	Air	Touch	Compassion	Heart, Blood, Circulatory system	Depression
THROAT Neck region	Thyroid	Ether	Hearing	Communication	Bronchial tubes, Vocal cords, Lungs	Lack of expression
BROW Between the eyes	Pituitary			Insight, Clarity	Lower brain, Left eye	Distorted thinking
CROWN Top of the head	Pineal			Higher Consciousness	Upper brain, Right eye	Loss of sense of self

For a number of reasons, the natural flow of subtle energy through the chakras can be disrupted and their rates of vibration thrown out of balance, so much so that we feel it as a blockage in a particular area. When we lay ourselves open to stress, through overwork and pressurized situations, allowing negative feelings to dominate our psychology, harboring wrong attitudes, not getting proper physical and mental rest, or taking in food and drink unsuited to our bodies, we are placing the chakras under duress, demanding that they mediate more energy than they can handle. Sound medicine in the form of vocal toning can help to retune them, restoring balance in the process because the resonances of the voice can alter the vibrational rates of these wheels. When the toning is effective, the sensation is that blockages of energy, at whatever point along the route of the chakras, have been removed.

There is no one definitive system of vocal toning of the chakras, that is, no system of particular frequencies in combination with the consonant/vowel sounds that guarantees success for all individuals. The best-known system of the East is Tantra Yoga (also known as Kundalini Yoga) and in the West there are several methods which have as their basis changing vowel frequencies. Nor is there a universal system that links musical tones to the seven chakras, such as relating the chakras to the seven tones of the C major scale—C D E F G A B—a system commonly offered. Furthermore, there is no scientific proof that there is a particular set of chakra frequencies for all human beings.* Even if there were, some or all might lie outside the human vocal range. When working alone, individuals have to explore their sound space and, according to their perceived vibrational patterns, select the seed syllables and tones—in the form of a scale or otherwise—that have the desired effect. On the other hand, group work needs to have an agreed system, usually established by the intuition and experience of the workshop leader. One practical consideration is the range of voices when using different

---

* A mathematically based system for chakra frequencies called Prima Sounds has been calculated and developed by an Austrian professor and an American musician. See resources under "Prima Sounds."

scales. Therefore the multiple voices of a group ultimately rely more on the changing consonant/vowel vibrations than any particular set of tones.

As always, follow the general instructions about preparing for toning. For example, the toning of the chakras could be carried out while standing, sitting, or lying down. In deciding what musical tones, or frequencies, you will use, choose from the following methods according to your ability to find specific tones by whatever means:

1. Remain on the same tone for all the chakras. Ideally, this would be your fundamental tone. If not, use any resonant tone in the low to middle range of your voice.

2. Change the tones intuitively, starting on a fairly low tone and proceeding to higher ones with each succeeding chakra. Move upward easily so as not to exceed your pre-established vocal range. It is generally accepted that the frequencies are higher as you move upward through the seven chakras. This is indicated in the Yogic tradition in which the chakras are described as having increasing numbers of petals. If selecting just one chakra to tone, your intuition will have to guide you. As with discovering your fundamental tone, you could use a tape recorder for remembering a tone that worked well for a particular chakra.

3. Change the tones systematically using either the major, overtone, or pentatonic scales. These scales with their twelve transpositions are presented in chapter 7. Choose a starting note that will help to produce a resonant scale that fits well into your vocal range. For example, the scales of A and B major might both fit your range well but you may sense that the A scale provides more resonance. If toning just one chakra, you would have to equate its number with the corresponding scale step. For example, if working with the F major scale, you would tone on the note C for the throat chakra because the throat is the fifth one up and C is the fifth note of the F major scale. If using the pentatonic

scale, the C is the fourth note and thus corresponds to the heart chakra.

4. Using these same scales, start on your fundamental tone. This may not be practical because the fundamental might push you out of your vocal range and not provide you with sufficient resonance. For example, a man might have D as his fundamental tone, seven tones down from middle C. However, he might be unable to rise all the way through the seven notes. In this situation it is suggested that someone wanting to incorporate the fundamental tone should begin a perfect fifth lower. To do this, find your fundamental tone in the fifth column for the major and overtone scales and the fourth column for the pentatonic scale (pages 63–64) and move backward to the note in the first column. So the person with the fundamental note of D would use G as the starting point as follows:

1	2	3	4	5	6	7	
G	A	B	C	D	E	F#	Major
G	A	B	C#	D	E	F	Overtone
G	A	B	D	E	G	A	Pentatonic

For group work, the author in his workshops favors both intuitively and rationally the pentatonic scale starting on F.* This is the most universal of scales and forms the basis of the great Chinese music tradition with its attendant philosophy. Chinese musical theorists have set the foundation tone of Chinese music, known as *huang chung* and trans-

---

* This scale arises out of a series of rising perfect fifth intervals (F C G D A) which are rearranged into scale order within an octave. These intervals, according to Chinese musical theory, continue in an ever ascending spiral ad infinitum, creating innumerable frequencies. At the thirteenth tone in the series they overshoot the distance of seven octaves by a fraction known as the Pythagorean comma. Thus, the pentatonic scale is at the basis of a system that can be described as transcendental. See Alain Danielou, *Music and the Power of Sound* (Rochester, Vt.: Inner Traditions, 1995), 29–57.

lated as "yellow bell," as F.[2] The Chinese connect this with the element Earth which aligns itself with the root chakra. Perhaps the greatest musical work inspired by Mother Nature, the Earth, is the "Pastoral" symphony of Beethoven written in the key of F major. In traditional Indian classical music, the fourth tone of its basic scale (roughly equivalent to F as it relates to the Western C major scale) is given the syllable MA, a seed sound that is associated with *mater* or "mother," the feminine generative principle.

The five-tone scale misses out two tones as it moves through the space of an octave—F G A C D—B and E are missing. The result is that the fourth tone is C, corresponding to the centerpoint of the chakra design, the heart. For the westerner, C is also the centerpoint in defining musical structure. The first note that someone is taught at the piano is middle C and the C major scale consists of only white notes. This then produces the musical interval known as the perfect fifth between F (the root chakra) and C (the heart chakra). All great musical cultures of the world respect the sacredness of this combination as it represents the first differentiation in the overtone series, numbers 2 and 3 (see chapter 12). The sound healer John Beaulieu, in describing the effects of his tuning forks, states that Lao-tzu described this interval as the sound of universal harmony between the forces of Yin and Yang and that it is the sound through which the Indian deity *Shiva* calls *Shakti* (the female principle of generative power) to the dance of life, as well as the sound which Apollo, the Greek god of music and healing, plucked on his sacred lyre to call dolphin messengers to Delphi.[3] The feeling inherent in this interval is one of profound stability and peace. Thus, we can rest in this perfect fifth sound of F and C as though floating in the lightness of air. For air is the element associated with the heart chakra.

The pentatonic scale also contains a correlation between the root (F) and brow (F), and the sacral (G) and crown (G) chakras because the first two notes of the pentatonic scale are repeated an octave higher (twice the frequency) to make seven tones. This extension of the scale produces two further harmonious perfect fifth intervals between the sacral (lower G), which equals creativity, and the throat (D), which equals communication, and the heart (C), which is compassion, and the crown (upper G), which is the state of unconditional love and happiness. Finally, in surpassing the octave, the upper G symbolizes moving into the next realm of expanding consciousness in a never-ending ascending spiral.

The complete system is as follows:

CHAKRA	TONE	SYMBOLIC WORD
Root	F	Foundation
Sacral	G	Genesis
Solar Plexus	A	Affirmation
Heart	C	Compassion
Throat	D	Declaration
Brow	F (octave above root)	Foresight
Crown	G (octave above sacral)	Godhead

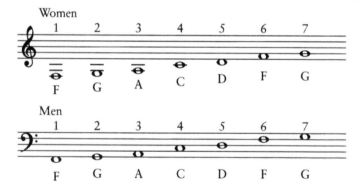

There are two essential systems of consonant/vowel seed syllables for toning the chakras: from the East, the Tantra Yoga tradition of India, and from the West, as developed by sound-healing practitioners, the ascending frequency of a vowel sound system. In the former, the differentiation among the first five chakras is found in the change of the opening consonant. A mnemonic to help remember the order of the five consonants is "Let Venus Rule Your Heart." The central vowel sound of AH, a constant referral to the heart center, and the succeeding MMM remain the same. Thereafter the pattern discontinues with the use of OM for the brow chakra and silence (beyond sound) for the crown. Alternatively, the crown could be toned by sounding a prolonged humming MMM. The Western system presented here uses the ascending frequency vowels and joins to them the Tantra Yoga system of changing consonants and the all important closing MMM. Through intuition, the author has added the consonants S and K for the brow and crown chakras respectively.

CHAKRA	TANTRA YOGA	ADAPTED WESTERN
Root	Lam (LL AH MMM)	Lum (LL UH MMM)
Sacral	Vam (VV AH MMM)	Voom (VV OO MMM)
Solar Plexus	Ram (RR AH MMM)	Raum (RR AW MMM)
Heart	Yam (YY AH MMM)	Yam (YY AH MMM)
Throat	Ham (HH AH MM)	Haim (HH AYE MMM)
Brow	Om (OOO MMM)	Sim (SS EYE MMM)
Crown	MMMMMMM*	Keem (K EEE MMM)

* According to the Tantra Yoga system, the seed mantra for the crown chakra is beyond sound. This has been represented by the absence of any vowel, retaining only a humming of the final MMM.

TONING ALONE

As always there is a choice between standing up, sitting, or lying down. When sitting, remember to use an upright chair that supports your back and allows your feet to touch the floor. Place your slightly cupped hands in your lap, palms up as if receiving. If standing, assume a stable position with feet apart and arms relaxed at your side. Or the hands can be held at the heart joined together in a prayer position. If lying down for any length of time, use a small pillow to support the head and, if need be, a light blanket to keep warm. The hands can also be used to direct the sound to the corresponding chakra. In this case, lightly place the hands approximately in the position of each chakra to be toned. For the throat chakra, the easiest position is cupping your hands under the jaw. For the brow, put the palms over the closed eyes with fingers extending over the brow. For the crown, put the palms just above the ears with the fingers extending over the top of the head. The eyes will be closed as you also mentally direct the toning to each chakra. If using a keyboard or tape recorder to find notes, put them in an easily reachable position.

The actual toning is to be done slowly and rhythmically. One approach is to work with sets of five, the first four receiving two pulses each (a pulse about 1 second or slightly slower) and the fifth, with the elongated MMM, receiving four pulses. Take a quick breath at the end of a cycle or an extra breath before the fifth repetition. The final MMM could be extended for longer if you wish. For example:

LAM	LAM	LAM	LAM	LA-	MMM
2	2	2	2	1	3

LUHM	LUHM	LUHM	LUHM	LUH-	MMM
2	2	2	2	1	3

Emphasize the opening consonant through slight exaggeration. This is important because the sounds are directed to the different chakras through the consonants as given in the Tantra Yoga tradition. Think of the threefold aspect of each seed syllable or mantra as pieces of fruit from which you want to extract as much juice as possible. As shown above, extend the MMM sound at the end of the cycle which deepens the process and leads to a natural pause, if desired. If toning all seven chakras, spend about 3–4 minutes on each.

There is no need to tone all seven chakras each time you engage in this sound ritual. As noted earlier, you can choose to tone only those that relate to a specific physical or emotional condition that needs to be healed. If you choose to do a few, it is best not to go beyond 30 minutes in total. For just one chakra, tone for a maximum of 10 minutes.

TONING WITH A PARTNER

Sit in comfortable chairs opposite each other so that your hands can touch. It might require that the legs of one person be between the other in some manner. Rest the hands on the legs so the arms do not become tired. One of you arrange your hands so that one palm is up, the other down, with your partner doing the reverse. In the toning, allow the two voices to merge as much as possible. Remain focused on which chakra is being toned.

Alternatively, one person can lie down, hands at their sides, on the floor, a bed, or a practitioner's table. Use a pillow to support the head. The partner, either standing or kneeling alongside, lightly places his or her hands on either side of the chakra to be toned up until the fourth (the heart). For the last three, stand, sit, or kneel behind your partner's head. For the throat, place your hands on the upper chest near the throat; for the brow, over the forehead; and for the crown, cradle the head in the palms of your hands. Where possible, direct your toning directly into each chakra in turn. The one receiving the therapeutic touch should also join in with the toning.

SUPPLEMENTAL CHAKRA TONING

A complementary approach to toning the chakras is to concentrate on the consonants with some additional vowel sounds. This gives a greater focus to the initial vibration in the Tantra Yoga tradition. Ensure that as much of the sonic juice of each consonant is squeezed from it through prolongation and exaggeration. Each one is accompanied by T'ai Chi–like movements to bring a greater intention to the healing work. If doing the entire set, spend about 3–5 minutes on each chakra. If concentrating on one or two, 10 minutes is sufficient.

1. ROOT

Sound: UL-UL-UL-UL (etc.) -LAH

Using a deep yet resonant tone in your voice, create a strong rhythmic pulsing of the UL about one a second or slightly slower. The LAH occurs at the end of the movement. It is sounded vigorously, then falling away as in a sigh.

Movement: Left foot forward, right foot behind and turned outward at roughly a 90 degree angle to the left. This foot position can be reversed. Begin with hands at your sides. Lean forward only as far as your body will allow, letting the hands move toward the floor in front of you as though you are going to scoop up the earth. Lift your hands holding the earth while bringing the body back to the erect position. The movement ends when the two hands are palm up alongside the head, the head is uplifted, and the front foot is partially lifted off the floor with the heel touching. All during the movement the UL sounds are pulsed until the very endpoint when the LAH is intoned as described above. Hold the position for about 20 seconds, mentally breathing in the UL and breathing out the LAH through the nose. From the concluding hand position descend once again, front foot back on the floor, to dig into the earth and continue more cycles.

2. SACRAL

Sound: VIV-VIV-VIV-VIV

Any good note in your voice is acceptable. The sound is somewhat like an insect. Keep the lips close to each other feeling their tingling and vibration. Sound the VIV rapidly (about four per second), taking breath as is needed. At the end of each cycle let the sound fade away.

Movement: Normal standing position with the feet balancing the body and the knees relaxed. Hold the hands palms down alongside the body at the level of the sacral region—roughly the waistline—and two inches away from the body. Move the hands forward as though the fingers are going to join in front. Just before they meet, point the fingers outward so you form the prayer position, hands about an inch apart. As the hands come away from the body, turn the palms downward and move the hands away from one another, keeping them in the plane of the sacral region. This final part is an arc-like movement of each hand as it returns to its original position. The VIV seed syllable will be intoned throughout the movement and fade as described above. At the end of each cycle pause and listen to the sound mentally, still feeling it on your lips. Allow gaps between cycles of about 10 seconds.

3. SOLAR PLEXUS

Sound: ER-ER-ER-ER (etc.) -RAH

Use a comfortable note in your voice and create a slowly pulsating, vigorous ER (as in "error") as if you are frustrated. RAH is intoned with equal vigor at the end of a cycle and then allowed to slide downward as the breath fades.

Movement: Begin with your hands at your sides, palms facing to the rear. Lift your hands outward and move them slightly behind you on the ascent. At the solar plexus level pull the hands in front of the body in a kind of circular movement. As your hands meet in front of you the palms will turn upward at the solar plexus level. Throughout this movement, thus far, the ER syllable is repeated. When palms are presented it is with a small, outward thrust as though you are throwing off stale energy. In conjunction with the thrust the RAH is intoned as described.

Hold this palms up position, breathing in the ER and out with the RAH mentally for about 20 seconds and then resume the cycles. In resuming allow the hands to fall with the palms gradually facing to the rear as before.

4. HEART

Sound: YAH-YOU

Each of these seed syllables is begun by stretching the Y sound for a few seconds before changing to the vowel. The starting note is to be relatively high without strain. However, as soon as the vowel appears let the sound slide down as in a siren and with a yearning, crying out quality. This also gives your bodies, visible and invisible, a multiplicity of frequencies.

Movement: Begin in the usual standing position, feet under the shoulders and knees relaxed. Hold the right hand in the form of a fist over the heart region and place the open left hand over the right without touching. With the fist strike the sternum with moderate force three times—this is a point of stimulation for the thymus gland, which is linked to the immune system. This is a gesture of opening the heart. Visualize that the ensuing sounds are pouring out from this opening. Opening the right hand, turn and separate your hands as though you are holding an expanding ball of energy above your head, palms facing each other. Lift your head so as to look at the ball. As you open up in this way sound the YAH. At its completion pause for a few seconds. Then, with the sounding of the YOU in the same manner, let the arms fall in a curvature as though there is a very large person before you that you want to embrace and hold to your heart. Move the hands to the heart, right hand touching the body with left over it. In the silence between cycles mentally breathe in the YAH and out the YOU for 20–30 seconds before resuming the cycles beginning with the striking of the breast.

5. THROAT

Sound: HAH

This is done completely on the breath as it is the sound of H that is its essence.

Movement: In the usual standing position, hold out the arms fully extended with palms down, the hands at roughly a 45 degree angle to the floor. On the long inbreath slowly pull back the hands to about six inches from the shoulders. Keeping an open throat push out the sound of the breath HAH, cleansing this chakra, and at the same time slowly push the hands back to their original position. There is no need for pauses. Just maintain the pattern in a steady rhythm.

6/7. BROW/CROWN

Sound: MMMMMM (humming)

To give the humming sound a brightness and get it to move up into the head region, put a smile on your face and imagine the upward curve of the mouth as the means for the ascending sound.

Movement: This can be done either standing or sitting. Place the fingers of your hands on the head as follows: thumbs on the upper cheeks, first and second fingers just above the eyebrows, ring fingers on the point between the brows, and pinky fingers on the bridge of the nose. When initiating the M sound momentarily put a slight pressure on the brow chakra with the ring fingers. During the humming move the hands up and away from the head as though the head were expanding. Allow the hands to float above the head where they form a prayer position, not touching. Taking breath as you need it and still sounding the MMM, pull the hands down, just grazing the hair and move them back to the original position. At the points between cycles follow your breath through the nose for a short while.

COLLECTIVE SPONTANEOUS TONING

This ritual closely follows that of collective improvised singing described in chapter 10. Once again the group gathers in a close circle with arms around each other's waists. The group selects a particular vowel, usually AH, OH, or OO. After a count of three the members immediately send out their various tones. As this interplay unfolds, the object is to tune the circuit, allowing the voices to gravitate into a harmonious steady state sound. This can take the form of a single tone to which the members are intuitively drawn. It becomes, in effect, the group tone and can be used subsequently for other group work. Or the sounds can assume the shape of a simple consonant major chord or triad, often called the chord of Nature as it is found early on in the third octave of the overtone series (see chapter 12). The coalescing of the group in either way unites the members profoundly and leads them into a deep state of meditation. In such a state they should be able to intuit when to discontinue the sound and then remain standing in silence. Gentle bell sounds are best for bringing the meditation to a conclusion.

TONING SEED SYLLABLES

Using the systems above as a model for toning the chakras, a sonic language of seed syllables can be created that directs itself to two or three energy centers. These seed syllables become, in effect, tailor-made to your needs. They can start with a consonant, followed by a vowel, and possibly end with another consonant, often, but not necessarily, with MMM. The consonants and vowels would be limited to those presented for toning the chakras. As follows:

CONSONANTS: H   K   L   M   R   S   V   Y

VOWELS: UH (hug)   OO (food) OH (home) AW (awe) AH (father)

AYE (say)   EH (help)   EYE (sight)   EE (meet)

None of the combinations has to form a known word or have any meaning, unless you want to invest the created sound with a meaning. Its structure depends on which energy centers you want to stimulate. This approach is similar to that taught by the Native American Beautiful Painted Arrow in his book *Being and Vibration*. He states that any word can be made sacred and chanted as long as the meaning of the individual sounds and what their effect might be is understood.[4] Here are some examples:

L (root)	+ AYE (throat)	+ S (brow)
V (sacral)	+ AH (heart)	+ K (crown)
R (solar plexus)	+ OO (sacral)	+ MMM (all regions)
H (throat)	+ EE (crown)	+ R (solar plexus)
K (crown)	+ AH (heart)	+ MMM (all regions)

Let us explore the last example, which comes out as the word CALM. Its meaning is supposed to be about relaxation and the release of anxiety. Yet it begins with an explosive K sound unlike its sister words "psalm" and "balm" which are naturally soothing. In fact, in situations of duress, people will often say, "Keep calm," doubling the power of the K. So calmness is not just about being at peace, it is also about being fully awake and alert. It is a kind of dynamic state of relaxation in which you are prepared for any event.

The sound of CALM can be used to open up the heart. At first the K sound pierces through any hardheartedness. Then the AH sound resonates the heart's yearning for union and the MMM brings the deep peace and calm. As with keening presented in chapter 8, sound the K quite strongly without any vowel following it so that its shockwave carries down the spinal column to the gland linked with the heart, the thymus. This gland is an important center of our vitality. Its name derives from the Greek word *thymos* meaning "vitality." It plays an important role in maintaining the immune system, especially for the prevention of cancer. It has been demonstrated through kinesiological tests that knocking against the thymus with your fingertips or fist strengthens it and hence boosts your vitality.[5] This corresponds to the gesture of a religious person when asking for forgiveness (the opening up of the heart) and saying, "*mea culpa.*"

When sounding this potent seed syllable, add these movements:

The KALM Ritual

1. Stand as usual with the feet shoulder-width apart, knees in a relaxed position. Start with your hands uplifted and somewhat forward of the body, palms facing each other. While drawing in air using the deep-breathing technique, move your hands slowly toward the center of your chest, gradually closing the right hand into a relaxed fist. When the hands are about an inch away from the chest, strike the sternum firmly with the fist hand and at the same time sound the sharp K as though you desire to have the K pierce the heart.

2. Directly after producing the K sound, go into the AH followed by the prolonged MMM until your breath runs out. At the same time, open up your fist hand, move both hands downward and then outward drawing a circle in the air. In this there is a period of silence while you are breathing normally. When the circling hands reach the original position above and forward of the head, start the inbreath and move the hands once again toward the sternum. Continue the cycle for no more than 10 minutes. At the end sit down and enter the meditative state.

You are encouraged to experiment with consonant/vowel combinations to meet your needs in any healing process. Any work that opens us up and allows us to trust the intuition is to be welcomed. It is also possible that movements for these will arise out of your body spontaneously, and this should be allowed to develop.

TONING THE ORGANS OF THE BODY

Within the Chinese Taoist tradition there is a system of health maintenance and rejuvenation called the Healing Tao or Taoist Esoteric Yoga.[6]
Part of the practice involves the toning of healing sounds. Their purpose, with their complementary movements, is to dissipate any stresses,
tensions, or pain lodged in the organs. In essence they produce a release
of heat, a cooling down of the stressed areas. They can also be used for
ailments connected with the organs.* In all cases except the last (the
"Triple Warmer" on page 129), the toning is done in a chair that supports the back well. You place your full attention on the organ to be
toned so the sounds, psychologically speaking, are being directed there.

The table below sets out the correspondences between the organs,
their sounds, and related ailments. The movements are described
thereafter.

THE TAO SOUNDS

Organ	Physical Ailment	Psychological Disturbance	Sound
LUNGS	Asthma, Colds	Depression	Sssss
KIDNEY	Fatigue, Dizziness	Fear	Wooo(h)
LIVER	Digestive problems	Anger	Shhhh
HEART	Sore throat, Cold sores	Impatience	Haaaw
SPLEEN, STOMACH & PANCREAS	Nausea, Indigestion	Worry	Whoooo

---

* Another ancient Chinese system of toning various parts of the body called Tao Yin Fa,
requiring much more movement, is worth exploring. It is presented by the sound healer
Fabien Maman in his book *Raising Human Frequencies: The Way of Chi and the Subtle
Bodies*. See recommended reading.

General Instructions

Lungs

Sit in a straight-backed chair, legs slightly apart, and rest your hands, palms up, on your thighs. Slowly uplift the hands, following them with your eyes. Eyes can be open or shut. As the hands reach the top of your

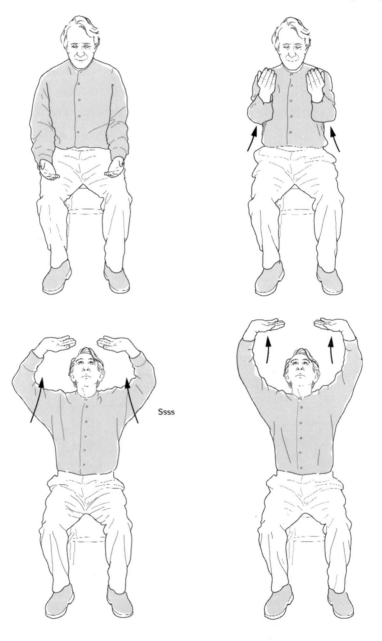

head, swivel them completely around so that the fingers are pointing toward each other, the palms facing up to the ceiling. Allow the hands to part so that they are approximately over the shoulders. This gives room for the chest to expand. As you uplift your hands, draw in breath as described in chapter 5. Then release the breath on a hissing SSSSS sound, the mouth nearly closed so the sound is covered yet inwardly intense, while pushing your hands up toward the ceiling. Push up as far as is comfortable, feeling an expansion of the chest. Remember that your attention is on the lungs and the eyes are still focused toward the hands so that the head is tilted well back. When the breath has been exhausted, slowly return the hands to their original position on your thighs while breathing normally. Once there, take a pause before repeating. Do no more than nine times.

Kidneys

Begin in the same position as for the lungs. Then draw your legs together, lean your body forward and clasp your hands around your knees. Slightly elevate the head while maintaining straight elbows. During this time draw in breath in the usual way. On the exhalation, make a very breathy WOOOH (as in WOE) sound as through whispered intensely. At the same time, fully contract the muscles of the abdomen towards the kidney region. On completion, slowly return to the original position described while breathing normally. Take a pause before repeating. Do no more than six times.

Liver

Sit in the normal position with your legs slightly apart and your hands on your thighs. Uplift the hands slowly, moving them slightly outward to draw a circle in the air. Allow the eyes to follow this movement peripherally so that the head is elevated. As your hands move toward each other to complete the circle above your head, interlace the fingers and then swivel the hands so that the palms face upward. Up to this

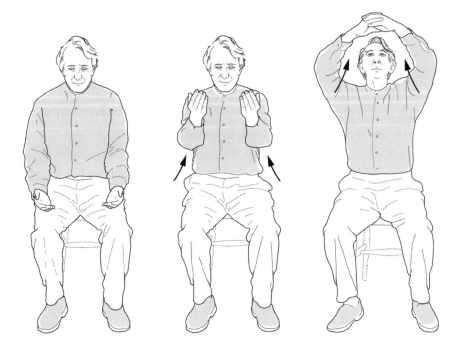

point there is a simultaneous drawing in of the breath in preparation for the sound. Keeping the fingers interlaced, push up the right palm to the ceiling. The eyes remain fixed on the hands. This is opening up the space for the liver on the right side of the body. With this pushing up, create an inwardly strong "Shhhh" like the sound of the ocean, the mouth fairly closed, and exhaust all your breath. Slowly return the hands to the thighs in reverse circular motion while breathing normally. Do no more than six times.

Heart

All the instructions for the liver apply to the heart except that the hands are reversed. The left palm pushes up to the ceiling. The sound produced is a very breathy "Haaaw," similar in effect to the WHO. Make certain that it is truly the AW vowel as in "ought."

Haaaw

Stomach/Pancreas/Spleen

Begin in the normal sitting position. Put your curved fingertips onto the body between the navel and the sternum, just off center to the left where the pancreas and spleen are located. Follow this with a deep inhalation. As you sound "Whooo" full of breath and from deep within the throat, push the fingertips easily into the region and simultaneously contract the abdominal muscles. On completion, return to normal breathing and place the hands on your thighs. Do no more than six times.

NOTE:

1. Between each cycle allow a gap of about 20–30 seconds while you focus your full attention on the organ in question.
2. If you are going to tone all five organs in succession, then do each one only three times.

There is a sixth location which is not officially an organ as defined by Western medicine. In Chinese medicine, it is connected with blood circulation and sexual energy and has been called the "triple warmer."

Triple Warmer

Lie down on your back. Use a pillow to support your head. This could be done on a bed as one of its benefits is to induce deep relaxation leading to sleep. Have your hands at the sides with the palms up and close your eyes. Draw in a deep breath. With the exhalation, produce a high-pitched sound of "Heeee" on the breath by baring your teeth. At the same time, work systematically with your muscles so that there is a sensation of your chest, solar plexus, and abdomen, in that order, being flattened. At the end of each cycle breathe normally, totally relax all those muscles and focus on what you feel to be the center of yourself. Do this exercise no more than six times.

12

Overtoning

All regularly vibrating sounds, most especially the human voice and musical instruments, consist of a fundamental tone that contains numerous higher frequencies called overtones, that is, they are tones above the fundamental produced. They are also referred to by musicians as harmonics and by physicists as partials. Normally the fundamental and its overtones are heard as one rich integrated sound. The overtone patterns can be likened to the DNA or genetic blueprint of the sound as they determine its quality, color, or timbre. The sounds of musical instruments are distinguished through the ascending overtone patterns. For example, a trumpet and a violin can sound the same fundamental tone or frequency of 256 cycles per second and yet the color of their sounds is utterly different. This is also true of human voices, so much so that voiceprints can be used to identify people for security purposes. This differentiation has to do with the strengths of the spectrum of the individual overtones or their absence. Overtones are taken for granted when we listen to voices and music. However, their existence is made known when they are absent or removed from a sound, for example, the absolute dullness of a sine-wave signal sent out by a TV station when not broadcasting or the computerized voices that give instructions at airports. On the other hand, we can clearly sense the overtones in the vocal sound of a singer like Luciano Pavarotti due to the richness of how he produces the vowels.

If the voice is a natural healing instrument, then the overtones are its aura, its bioenergetic field. They are what make sound organic—full of vitamins and minerals. At higher levels they can be likened to the music of angelic orders. It follows that the conscious production of overtones—that is, to make individual harmonics audible and hence to intensify them—increases the therapeutic capacity of the voice in certain respects. High-frequency sound in the form of overtones can be an agent for charging the cortex of the brain and therefore the central nervous system. Overtoning is a powerful form of centering the mind, decreasing the activity of the brainwaves, and the attention required to achieve clearly audible harmonics can lead into deep meditation.

In producing overtones with the voice it is best that the fundamental you choose be in your mid-range voice, beginning somewhere between the note C and the G just above it. For women, this is, as usual, middle C, and for the men, the C an octave below. Although it is an acoustical fact that the lower the fundamental the more overtones are possible, it is easier to hear the overtones when the fundamental is not too low. Determine which tone is best for your voice through experimenting. The chart on page 133 comprises the overtone series up to the tenth tone starting from the eight notes between C and the G above.

The following is a musical illustration of the overtone series beginning on C over the distance of four octaves:

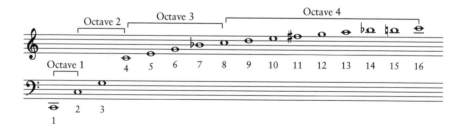

THE OVERTONE SERIES

1	2	3	4	5	6	7	8	9	10
C	C	G	C	E	G	Bb	C	D	E
Db	Db	Ab	Db	F	Ab	B	Db	Eb	F
D	D	A	D	F#	A	C	D	E	F#
Eb	Eb	Bb	Eb	G	Bb	Db	Eb	F	G
E	E	B	E	G#	B	D	E	F#	G#
F	F	C	F	A	C	Eb	F	G	A
Gb	Gb	Db	Gb	Bb	Db	E	Gb	Ab	Bb
G	G	D	G	B	D	F	G	A	B

Each of these rising series covers just over three octaves. Number 1 begins the first octave, number 2 the second octave, number 4 the third, and number 8 the fourth. These are given as a matter of interest but it is not necessary to know which number overtone you are producing. If that kind of knowledge is important to you, then seek the guidance of a teacher who specializes in overtoning techniques (see resources). Remember that much of voice work is intuitive. In this respect you will be experimenting, first by which fundamental you choose and then by allowing the overtones to emerge. Knowing which number overtone you are producing is a musical consideration and separate from feeling which overtone is effecting a healing resonance within you.

Because overtoning is a far more subtle form of therapeutic sound than ordinary toning, there needs to be some preliminary preparation. First of all, you need a good storehouse of breath and the ability to support it. For this, return to chapter 5 on breathing techniques and do some breath work before starting.

The following exercises are aids to having a relaxed jaw, tongue, and lips, all essential to overtone production.

Preliminary Exercises for Overtone Production

1. Begin with the gibberish and yawning exercises given in chapter 8 on natural sounds.

2. With quite an open mouth position, thereby relaxing the jaw, take a vowel sound starting low in your voice and sweep the sound upward as in a siren and then downward. Do it fairly slowly and on one breath. Keeping your arms loose, move them up and down in synchronization with the sweeping sound, either lifting them forward or out to the sides, whichever you prefer, so that at the top of the siren-vowel sound your hands are well above your head. Use the basic vowels of UH, OO, OH, AW, AH, AYE, EH, and EE and do each in turn. Naturally the shape of the mouth will alter for each one but nevertheless keep the mouth as wide open as is comfortable.

3. Choose a comfortable mid-range tone. Combine the consonant sound of Y with any two vowel sounds and say them back and forth in repeated quick succession and with exaggeration. This considerably loosens up the jaw and tongue. Examples: YAH-YOU, YEE-YOH, YOU-YAW, etc.

4. Similarly, for the loosening up of the lips, combine the consonant sound of M with vowels on a mid-range tone, either staying with one vowel over and over again or switching between two vowels. Keep the repetitions at a moderate speed. Examples: MOO, MOO, MOO, etc., or MAW, MAW, MAW, etc., or MA-MOO, MEE-MOH, MY-MAY, etc. This is quite a closed-mouth position. Only a small aperture is required and consequently your sound should not be loud. Exaggerate the lip movements. Push the sound upward into the nose so it is nasalized. Usually the MMM sounds throughout as a general

humming. Allow this to occur. Visualize the sound to be emanating from your nose. It sounds somewhat like a jaw harp and already provides aural glimpses of some overtones.

5. To open up the throat, follow the procedures of the Ging-Gang-Gung exercise given in chapter 5 incorporating the humming after-effect.

NOTE: In all the above cases, take in a deep breath and carry on the exercise until the breath is depleted. Take a small pause, breathe normally, and then resume.

OVERTONE PRODUCTION

Position Number 1

There are three basic positions of the mouth that will provide a good spectrum of vowels. In the first, which produces the lower overtones, the inside of the mouth is shaped as though a well-rounded tennis ball were placed inside. At the same time the throat is kept open by imagining the gargling-sound exercise. The tongue is placed down onto the lower palette and on the inside of the lower back teeth. Initially the lips are pushed slightly forward and shaped in a whistling position in order to produce the OH vowel. Nasalize the OH by focusing the breath up into the nose. Then, keeping the lips firm, move them slowly and vertically into a kind of smiling position. The vowel sound of OH will be altered and a small series of rising overtones will emerge. It is like saying the word WOW in slow motion. Reverse the lip movement and the overtones will descend. The word WHY can also be intoned by moving from a whistling position to a smiling position of the lips. The word WHY is particularly potent because it contains a wide spectrum of vowels from OOO to EEE. Thinking these particular sounds helps to project the overtones. The key point is that the words have to be slowly stretched out over a period of about 10 seconds. Then there is a chance to perceive the changes.

Position Number 2

A variation of the first position is as follows. The position of the mouth and the keeping of the open throat remain the same. Only the lip and tongue movements change. Start with the whistling position of the lips and sound out the word MORE . Begin by sounding the MMM first as an inner hum. Slowly push the lips forward, keeping them firm and imagining yourself imitating the face of a fish. Open up the aperture of the lips in the process as you move outward from the MMM into the ORRR sound. Again it is the nasalization, sending the sound up into the nasal cavity, that can project the overtones forward. Therefore the R sound has to be a twangy ERR as in the word ERROR. To achieve the ERR sound in MORE the tongue has to come forward and rise up to the roof of your mouth. You can then move up and down a series of overtones by moving the lips back and forth and moving the tongue up and forward and down and back, that is, changing between the MOH and ERR sounds.

Position Number 3

In this position the emission of the higher overtones can be achieved. A rounded inside of the mouth, the open throat, and the whistling lips are still essential. What is different is a greater movement of the tongue. A relaxed tongue is placed inside the upper teeth and then ever so slowly the tongue is slid back and forth along the upper palette as a way of changing from one overtone to another. A good single syllable word to experiment with is NEAR in a highly nasalized form. As before, the lips will be pushed forward in the manner of a fish. The N sound helps to get the nasal sound going. For this purpose give the NN a twang in your voice. Once the sound of the EAR part is established, keep a balance between the EEE vowel and the resonant buzz of the RR. Then slide the tongue back and forth for the changes. This sliding movement of the tongue occurs naturally in the sounding of the word WORRY (whirr-reee). Notice that the RR sound contributes considerably to the process and the lips have to move into the protruding position. In this case, the tongue begins at the back of the lower teeth, rises up to inside the upper teeth and finally moves forward toward the front teeth. This action gives a good spectrum of overtones from low to high. To slide from high to low, reverse the lip and tongue movements.

Finally, the three positions can be amalgamated, especially in relation to the tongue inside the lower teeth rising up and forward inside the upper teeth, to produce a full overtone spectrum. This can be effected by sounding out the three-syllable word: ORNERY (or-ner-ree) slowly and nasally, being aware of all the previous instructions.

As an aid to hearing the overtones it is very useful to cup your dominant ear (the right) with one hand, pushing the lobe forward, and place your slightly cupped other hand a few inches from your mouth. In this way the sounds are deflected off the cupped hand and sent directly into the dominant ear.

Once you have a reasonable mastery of these techniques, you can then have some control of the overtones to the point at which you can maintain a particular overtone that you sense has a special resonance within your body or psyche for healing purposes. Undoubtedly, much practice is necessary and the guidance of a teacher would be an added benefit.

SUMMARY

1. The support of the breath through the control of the abdominal muscles is essential in the projection of overtones. Do preliminary breathing exercises before creating overtones.

2. All parts of your vocal apparatus have to be put into a relaxed state, particularly the jaw, throat, and tongue.

3. Maintain the full rounded quality of the mouth cavity with firm lips.

4. Amplify the richness of the overtones by projecting the sound into the nasal cavity. Nasalization is very important.

5. To hear the overtones more clearly, use the technique of cupping your right ear and deflecting the overtones with your left hand placed in front of your mouth.

6. Keep the fundamental at a modest volume so that the overtones have a better chance to be heard. Do not let the fundamental sound produced overwhelm the overtones.

Notes

Chapter 1

1. Paul Hindemith, *A Composer's World: Horizons and Limitations* (New York: Doubleday & Co., 1961), 254.

Chapter 2

1. David Elkington, *In the Name of the Gods* (Sherborne, Dorset, UK: Green Man Press, 2001), 199.

2. Michael B. Green, "Superstrings," *Scientific American,* September 1986: 48–60.

3. Lyall Watson, *Supernature* (Garden City, N.Y.: Anchor Press, 1973), 90–96.

Chapter 3

1. John Beaulieu, *Music and Sound in the Healing Arts* (Barrytown, N.Y.: Station Hill Press, 1987), 53–74.

2. Hazrat Inayat Khan, *The Music of Life* (New Lebanon, N.Y.: Omega Publications, Inc., 1983), 94–5, 255.

Chapter 4

1. Lyall Watson, *Supernature* (Garden City, N.Y.: Anchor Press, 1973), 89–96.

Chapter 6

1. Further ideas about the nature of vowels and consonants and meaning can be found in *The Mystery of the Seven Vowels,* by Joscelyn Godwin (Grand Rapids, Mich.: Phanes Press, 1991); "The Power of Language," by Herbert Whone, in *Caduceus,* Issue 23, 1994: 20–23; *The Inner Nature of Music and the Experience of Tone,* by Rudolf Steiner (London: Rudolf Steiner Press, 1983), 31–9; *Form, Sound, Color and Healing,* by Theo Gimbel (Saffron Walden, U.K.: The C.W. Daniel Co., 1987), 59–61.

2. Hunbatz Men, *Secrets of Mayan Science/Religion* (Santa Fe, N. Mex.: Bear & Company Publishing, 1990), 89–90.

3. Mantak Chia, *Taoist Ways of Transforming Stress Into Vitality* (Huntington, N.Y.: Healing Tao Books, 1985), 61.

Chapter 8

1. P. D. Ouspensky, *In Search of the Miraculous* (New York and London: Harcourt Brace Jovanovich, 1977), 236.

2. For more information about the work of Dr. Adams, contact the Gesundheit Institute, 6248 Washington Boulevard, Arlington, VA 22205.

3. "Laughter," an article in the English newspaper *The Daily Mail* by Sheila Lavery on 17 February 1997.

4. Laurel Elizabeth Keyes, *Toning: The Creative Power of the Voice* (Marina del Rey, Calif.: De Vorss & Co, 1973), 108–9.

5. Joshua Leeds, "The Tomatis Method: Frequency Medicine for the 21st Century," *New Age Retailer* (August 1994). See also resources under "The Tomatis Method."

6. For further insights into the therapeutic use of humming, see Arden Mahlberg, "Getting the Ego Humming: Therapeutic Application of the Auditory Archetype 'M'," in *Music and Miracles* (Wheaton, Ill.: Quest Books, 1992), 219–229.

Chapter 10

1. For further information about this tradition refer to Laurence Freeman, OSB, *Christian Meditation: Your Daily Practice* (Rydalmere, NSW, Australia: Hunt & Thorpe, 1994).

Chapter 11

1. David V. Tansley, *Radionics & the Subtle Anatomy of Man* (Whitestable, U.K.: Health Science Press, 1976), 29.

2. See articles on Chinese music in *The New Grove Dictionary of Music and Musicians* (London: Macmillan, 1980).

3. John Beaulieu, *About BioSonic Repatterning*. See resources under "Tuning Forks."

4. Joseph Rael, *Being and Vibration* (Tulsa, Okla.: Council Oak Books, 1993), 144.

5. Bodo Baginski and Shalila Sharamon, *Reiki: Universal Life Energy* (Mendocino, Calif.: LifeRhythm Books, 1988), 83.

6. Mantak Chia, *Taoist Ways to Transform Stress Into Vitality* (Huntington, N.Y.: Healing Tao Books, 1985), 67–106. These practices are also cited in *Sounding the Inner Landscape* by Kay Gardner (see recommended reading). See also the other versions of the sounds described by Joseph F. Morales on the Web site www.baharna.com/chant/six__healing.htm.

Resources

SELECTED NON-VOCAL SOUND THERAPIES

Astrosonics

Originated in the early 1970s and developed extensively by Michael C. Heleus, astrosonics is the study of the relationship between the motion of planetary and other cosmic bodies to the Earth, rendered as sound. Through the realization of the characteristic sounds of the heavenly bodies, astrosonics is a method for making astrology experiential. The rendering of a person's birth chart as patterns of audible vibration awakens what already pre-exists within them, and hence, enables them to sense their life purpose and contribute to their spiritual unfoldment.

Michael C. Heleus
Astrosonic Services
2980 W. Foothill Drive
Phoenix, AR 85027
e-mail: mheleus1@cox.net

Bioacoustics (also known as Vibrational Retraining)

This sound therapy was discovered and developed by the American Sharry Edwards. It uses voice spectral analysis to identify and interpret frequency interactions within the body. Specifically, the voice is tested for pitch, octaves, and notes that are missing, non-harmonious, multi-plied, or broken. These particular notes in the form of low frequencies are then returned to the person's environment using a frequency generator. The missing frequencies are those needed to restore the body's health. As part of this therapy, correlation has been established between atomic weights, the orbit of planets, musical scale, and brainwaves.

Sound Health Research Institute
P.O. Box 416
Albany, OH 45701
Tel.: (740) 592-5115
Fax: (740) 592-6116
Web site: www.soundhealthresearch.org

Elaine Thompson/Robert Firkin
Vibrational Retraining
Glynswood House
32 St. Anne's Drive
Oldland Common
Bristol BS30 6RB
UK
Tel.: 01179 148683
Fax: 01179 873924
e-mail: elaine.thompson@ukonline.co.uk *or* robert.12@ukonline.co.uk
Web site: www.ukonline.co.uk/members/elaine.thompson

Cymatics

Developed out of the research of the Swiss scientist Hans Jenny (see recommended reading), who demonstrated in his many experiments that vibration has the power to shape matter according to the character of its substance. Cymatics (meaning "wave forms"), as taken up by its foremost practitioner Dr. Peter Guy Manners, is based on the principle that every cell, organ, muscle, and tissue resonates at its own particular frequency or sound pattern, and that when any of these lose their correct rate of vibration, illnesses and diseases will result. Dr. Manners has also calculated frequencies for particular ailments including problems at the mental level. Through the use of his specially designed Cymatic instrument, sets of frequencies matching those of the person's normal physical aspects are fed into the body; through the principle of resonance, the part of the body being treated will return to the correct frequency rate, and thus, to restored health.

Dr. Peter Guy Manners
The Bretforton Scientific & Medical Research Trust
Bretforton Hall Clinic
Bretforton near Evesham
Worcester W11 7JH
UK
Tel.: 01386 830537
Fax: 01386 830918
e-mail: info@cymatherapy.com
Web site: www.cymatics.org.uk

Electro-Crystal Therapy

Created and developed by Harry Oldfield, electro-crystal therapy is a method of diagnosis and treatment involving crystals, minerals, and gems that are electronically stimulated by various pulse repetition rates. The combination of pulsed high-frequency vibrations and crystals increases the range of healing. There has been a good success rate in treating many disorders, even up to the level of multiple sclerosis.

The School of Electro-Crystal Therapy
117 Long Drive
South Ruislip
Middlesex HA4 0HL
UK

Tel./Fax: 0208 8411716
e-mail: info@electrocrystal.com
Web site: www.electrocrystal.com

Gong Therapy

According to Don Conreaux, a prominent practitioner of gong therapy, the essential key to the gong's force of resonance and its effectiveness is the complete submersion and saturation of a person in layer upon layer of tone-cell multiplication. The universal gong sound is based upon the musical principle that all tones of equal amplitude keep resonating, adding to themselves to produce cumulative tone offspring, so to speak. This is a phenomenon unique to gongs and replicates exactly what happens in the building of the human physical, mental, emotional, and spiritual bodies.

Mysterious Tremendum
Box 318 Village Station
New York, NY 10014–0318
Tel.: (212) 715-6852
Fax: (212) 645-8159
e-mail: gongman@escape.com
Web site: www.holistic-resonance.com

Guided Imagery and Music

Originally researched and developed in the United States by Dr. Helen Bonny, GIM uses classical music and relaxation techniques to help patients access images at deep levels of consciousness. Used for a wide variety of applications in private practices and institutional settings, it offers relief from depression, stress-related and eating disorders, drug addiction, and physical and emotional abuse. It can also be applied for the purpose of exploring inner worlds and tapping into creativity.

The Bonny Method of Guided Imagery and Music
MAIA UK & IRELAND
Information Officer
Tel.: 01422 842 093
e-mail: maiauk@eggconnect.net

Association for Music and Imagery
P.O. Box 4286
Blaine, WA 98231–4286
Tel./Fax: (360) 756-8096
e-mail: ami@nas.com
Web site: www.bonnymethod.com/ami

International Lambdoma Research Institute (Barbara Hero)

The Lambdoma, shaped like the Greek letter lambda, is also known as the Pythagorean Table and is an infinity of musical ratios representing both the overtone and the undertone series. It is a profound musical model of the universe. The mathematician and visual artist Barbara Hero has studied this table for many years and invented a Lambdoma matrix keyboard which can project the sounds of these intervals both aurally and visually. She has produced a series of tapes containing the Lambdoma frequencies in different forms and believes through her experimentation that they have self-healing powers, particularly in resonating and balancing the chakras.

Barbara Hero
Founder/Director ILRI
496 Loop Road
Wells, ME 04090–7622
Tel./Fax: (207) 646-7950
e-mail: hero@cybertours.com
Web site: www.lambdoma.com

Monochord Table

Invented by Joachim Marz, a clinical music therapist at the University of Basle, the monochord table is a kind of musical instrument built in the shape of a table, its barrel-shaped resonance box lined with numerous strings tuned to the perfect fifth of D and A. It is designed so that the vibrations of specific harmonies and overtones permeate the bodies of those lying on the table and envelop their senses in a healing environment. It has been used in a great variety of ways from mothers experiencing difficult pregnancies to stressed business executives. A recording of monochord music entitled "Monochord Music" on the Village Life label has been produced by the British musician Sonia Slany (www.jazzcds.co.uk/soniaslany).

Joachim Marz
Dorf Strasse 40
5326 Schwaderlauch
SWITZERLAND
Tel.: 00 41 56 250 3117
Fax: 00 41 56 250 3116
e-mail: j.marz@gmx.ch

Tibetan Singing Bowls

Tibetan singing bowls, consisting of five, seven, and sometimes nine metals, are made of different thicknesses that produce a variety of tones and harmonics. A bowl is sounded with a wooden wand by either rubbing around the rim or stroking the side. In a general way, they have been used as a sound massage, establishing in people a deep sense of relaxation and peace, and have been applied to people with physical and mental handicaps within the context of music therapy. At a deeper level, the pulsations of the tones set off harmonics that penetrate the aura and the chakra centers. This process changes the recipient's state of consciousness to the slower rates of Alpha and Theta waves in which specific healing can take place. The great master of the art of playing these bowls for therapeutic purposes is Frank Perry whose contact details are:

Frank Perry
3 Drake Close
Ringwood
Hants BH24 1UG
UK
Tel.: 01425 470168
e-mail: Frank@frankperry.co.uk
Web site: www.frankperry.co.uk

The Tomatis Method

Named after the French neurologist and ear specialist, Professor Alfred Tomatis, this is a method of listening to specially filtered sound that has positive effects in the treatment of learning difficulties, poor concentration and memory, psychological depression, chronic fatigue, tinnitus, immune dysfunction, and generally increases the capacity of brain functions. It has proved very effective with children. It is based on the principle that the primary role of the ear is to charge the neo-cortex of the brain, and thus, the total nervous system. Dr. Tomatis has noted that it is the higher frequencies of a mother's voice that nourish her child while in the womb. Thus, for example, the high-frequency end of the sound spectrum of certain music, such as that of Mozart and Gregorian chant, is employed in this therapy. In effect it is a comprehensive method for retraining the ear. There are Tomatis Centers worldwide. Two of these from whom other centers could be contacted are:

The Listening Centre (UK)
Maltings Studio
16A Station Street
Lewes

East Sussex BN7 2DB
UK
Tel.: 01273 474877
Fax: 01273 487500
e-mail: enquiries@listeningcentre.co.uk
Web site: www.listeningcentre.co.uk

The Center for Inner Change
5655 S. Yosemite Street
Suite 206
Greenwood Village, CO 80111
Tel.: (303) 320-4411
Fax: (303) 322-5550
e-mail: info@centerforinnerchange.com
Web site: www.centerforinnerchange.com

Tuning Forks

The principal proponent of the use of tuning forks for healing is John
Beaulieu, a polarity therapist and musician, who calls the process
"biosonic repatterning." The forks that he has had designed are tuned
to precise mathematical proportions known as the Pythagorean tuning.
They emit such a purity of sound with concurrent overtones that they
induce a fine state of centering and deep relaxation. As he describes it,
"In listening to these intervals (a combination of two tuning forks) an
archetypal resonance is created resulting in a physical and psychic
repatterning of our mind, bodies, and spirit." The intervals are also cor-
related to the elements of earth, water, fire, and air and can help to
stimulate and increase the influence of a particular element within a
person.

BioSonic Enterprises
P.O. Box 487
High Falls, NY 12440
Tel.: (800) 925-0159
e-mail: sales@biosonics.com *or* john@biosonics.com
Web site: www.biosonics.com

SELECTED SPECIFIC VOICE THERAPIES

Music Thanatology

Music for the dying, or music thanatology as it has been coined by its founder Therese Schroeder-Sheker, is a form of music therapy that is solely concerned with the many and varied needs of the dying. Its chief purpose is to enable a dying person to move toward the portal of death so that nothing prevents or impedes them from passing on in as serene a state as possible. To this end the practitioner sings primarily hymns, antiphons, sequences, psalms, and litanies of early Christian plainsong accompanied by the harp. A school for this therapy entitled The Chalice of Repose Project has been established by its founder.

The Chalice of Repose Project, Inc.
P.O. Box 169
Mt. Angel, OR 97362-0169
Tel.: (503) 845-6089
e-mail: corpinfo@chaliceofrepose.org
Web site: www.chaliceofrepose.com

Overtoning

There are many approaches to the healing process through overtoning. Three important exponents and teachers of overtoning are David Hykes, Rollin Rachele, and Jill Purce. For contact details of Rachele and Purce, see the next section "Selected Compact Discs/Cassette Tapes/Videos." Hykes's contact details are given below.

David Hykes
Harmonique Centre
Pommereau
41240 Autanville
FRANCE
Tel.: (33) 254 72 82 12
Web site: www.harmonicworld.com

Harmonic Presence Foundation (USA)
c/o Stone Ridge Center for the Arts
Route 209
Stone Ridge, NY 12484
Tel.: (845) 687-8890

For more information on European overtone practitioners I recommend obtaining the "*Caduceus* Resource Guide to Overtone Singing" prepared by Brian Lee.

Caduceus
38 Russell Terrace
Leamington Spa
Warwickshire CV31 1HE
UK
Tel.: 01926 451897
Fax: 01926 885565
e-mail: caduceus@caduceus.info
Web site: www.caduceus.info

Voice Movement Therapy

Pioneered by Paul Newham, the author of *The Singing Cure: An Introduction to Voice Movement Therapy*, its method is based on the premise that everyone's voice is a blueprint of their underlying states; that stress and pain and despair can be detected through such aspects of the voice as tonal range, timbre, mode of delivery, and use of the breath. In particular, the singing voice is seen as the conveyor of concealed thoughts and unexpressed feelings and imaginings. By reclaiming and empowering the voice, physical and mental stress can be relieved and self-esteem can consequently be uplifted. Movement is used to complement the vocal work and to encourage the release of the vocal sounds.

International Association of Voice Movement Therapy
P.O. Box 34346
London NW6 1ZA
UK
e-mail: info@iavmt.org
Web site: www.iavmt.org

ORGANIZATIONS

The Association of Sound Therapy and Harmonic Studies

The founders of this association, Nestor Kornblum and Michele Averard, conduct courses dealing with the therapeutic uses of sound, especially the voice and, in particular, overtone singing. These take place in a specially built, magnificent sound dome, 100 yards in diameter. They offer an overtone instruction tape in Spanish.

The Association of Sound Therapy and Harmonic Studies
Sound Journey
Carrer del Mig 1
Alcalali 03728
Alicante
SPAIN
Tel.: 00 34 96 648 2312
e-mail: shamael@arrakis.es
Web site: www.arrakis.es/~shamael

Caduceus *Sound Healing Conferences*

Under the editorship of Sarida Brown, the journal *Caduceus* (subtitled "Healing into Wholeness") has taken a specific interest in the subject of sound healing. In 1999 it presented the first conference in England on healing with sound and music. Many of its issues contain articles on the subject with Issue 23 (1994) devoted entirely to it. *Caduceus* has produced both a *Sound Healing Resource Guide* and a *Guide to Overtone Singing*, both available from:

Caduceus
38 Russell Terrace
Leamington Spa
Warwickshire CV31 1HE
UK
Tel.: 01926 451897
Fax: 01926 885565
e-mail: caduceus@caduceus.info
Web site: www.caduceus.info

Sound Healers Association

Founded in 1982 by the leading therapeutic sound practitioner Jonathan Goldman, this non-profit-making organization is dedicated to research and awareness of the uses of sound and music as therapeutic and transformational modalities. Among its many activities, it offers Healing Sounds seminars and correspondence courses and publishes an international directory and resource guide that contains articles, interviews, and a bibliography. The listings are primarily based in the United States.

Sound Healers Association
P.O. Box 2240
Boulder, CO 80306
Tel.: (303) 443-8181

Fax: (303) 443-6023
e-mail: info@healingsounds.com
Web site: www.healingsounds.com

Healing Music Association

This is an organization of people who utilize sound and music in the healing arts. The purpose of this association is to promote education, scientific study, and a sense of community for people who share their experiences and knowledge about sound and music in healing.

e-mail: amrita@healingmusic.org
Web site: www.healingmusic.org

Healing Sound and Music Colloquiums

These conferences are the brainchild of Jeff Volk, director of Lumina Productions, and have been held each year in the United States from 1993 to 1998. They have brought together a wide-ranging array of leading experts in the sound-therapy field including Don Campbell, Jonathan Goldman, Jill Purce, John Beaulieu, Kay Gardner, Barbara Hero, Fabien Maman, Vicki Dodd, Valerie Hunt, Steven Halpern, and Therese Schroeder-Sheker. Many of the talks given over the years are available on cassette tapes. Volk has also produced two videos on sound-healing modalities and issued three videos on the work of Hans Jenny.

Lumina Productions
219 Grant Road
Newmarket, NH 03857
Tel.: (603) 659-2929
Fax: (603) 659-2939
e-mail: jeffvolk@nh.ultranet.com
Web site: www.cymaticsource.com

The Natural Voice Practitioners' Network

The network is a resource for voice work practitioners in the United Kingdom. It provides a range of opportunities for people to explore their voices and enjoy song, including voice and song workshops, training, short courses, creative projects, and community choirs.

Suzanne Chawner, administrator
The Natural Voice Practitioners' Network
Tel.: 44 01923 444440
e-mail: Admin@naturalvoice.net
Web site: www.naturalvoice.net

Tama Do: The Academy of Sound, Color, and Movement

This academy was founded by the musician, composer, acupuncturist, and bioenergetician Fabian Maman who draws upon Chinese philosophy and medicine in his sound therapy work and research. For example, he has linked music and acupuncture through the use of tuning forks. He has produced a series of four books on these subjects (see recommended reading).

The Academy of Sound, Color, and Movement
2060 Las Flores Canyon Road
Malibu, CA 90265
Tel.: (800) 615-3675
e-mail: info@tama-do.com *or*
tamadoacademy@aol.com (outside U.S.)
Web site: www.tama-do.com

Tonalis—Center for the Study and Development of Music

This center, founded by Michael Deason-Barrow in 1991, offers workshops and long-term courses in community music-making, world music in education, and music as a healing art. These courses explore the therapeutic application of rhythm, tone, dynamics, phrase, improvisation, and new musical instruments, as well as the fundamental freeing of the voice. A key aim is to create bridges between musicians on different musical paths so they can meet and learn from each other—for example, amateurs and professionals, classical and world music practitioners, university researchers, and those exploring the sacred mysteries of music.

Tonalis
4 Castle Farm Close
Leighterton, Gloucestershire GL8 8UY
UK
Tel.: 01666 890460
e-mail: tonalis@aol.com
Web site: www.tonalismusic.com

SELECTED COMPACT DISCS/CASSETTE TAPES/VIDEOS

"Atlantean Chants" (2-CD set)

These are a set of thirty-six short chants (eighteen on CD-1 and eighteen on CD-2) which were channeled into the consciousness of the internationally known spiritual teacher Frank Alper. Explanations of the meaning and purpose of the chants, which were a part of the spiritual tradition of the lost continent of Atlantis, are revealed in his three books *Exploring Atlantis I-III* (see recommended reading). The CDs and the books are available from:

Adamis Enterprises International
SWITZERLAND
Tel./Fax: 0041 10341630 33 01
Web site: www.adamis.ch

"Cymatics: The Healing Nature of Sound" (80-min. video)

Dr. Peter Guy Manners describes how audible sound can be employed as a healing modality and demonstrates the Cymatic Applicator which he developed for this purpose. The video includes an interview with Jonathan Goldman and the video "Cymatics: Bringing Matter to Life with Sound" listed below.

"Cymatics: Bringing Matter to Life With Sound" & "Cymatics: SoundScapes" (2 30-min. videos)

Highlights of Dr. Hans Jenny's pioneering experiments using audible sound to excite inert substances into lifelike, flowing forms. These delicate and intricate patterns demonstrate how matter is responsive to its underlying vibrational tone.

"Of Sound Mind and Body: Music and Vibrational Healing" (70-min. video)

Produced by Jeff Volk, this video explores the many ways in which music, sound, and vibration influence every aspect of our being. Its content is highly visual and dramatic and provides a wealth of detailed information presented by many of the leading figures in the field of sound therapy as it relates to mind–body medicine.

"Sounding the Psyche: Attuning the Bodymind" (90-min. video)

This video examines a variety of sound practices ranging from ancient Sanskrit chanting to contemporary innovations in vibrotactile therapies and psycho-acoustic technologies. Featuring the pioneering work of Dr. Alfred Tomatis, Dr. Hans Jenny, and Robert Monroe (The Monroe Institute), this video shows not only how sound structures matter, but how specialized vibrational frequencies can alter consciousness.

These five videos are available from:
MACROmedia
219 Grant Road
Newmarket, NH 03857
Tel.: (603) 659-2929
Fax: (603) 659-2939
e-mail: jeffvolk@nh.ultranet.com
Web site: www.cymaticsource.com

"Healing Sounds Instructional CD"

A companion recording to Jonathan Goldman's book *Healing Sounds* (see recommended reading). It deals with vowels as mantras and the fundamentals of vocal harmonics.

"Sacred Gateways" (CD)

This recording has a selection of well-known chants from different sources. They are intoned by a group of men led by Jonathan Goldman and accompanied by simple drumming. It includes Hey Yungua, Om Mani Padme Hum, En Lak'Ech, Om Nama Shivaya, Kodosh/Allah Hu, and Spirit of the Sound.

"Chakra Chants" (CD)

This CD was created to resonate and align the energy centers of the body known as the chakras. The sounds are designed to create balance in the physical, emotional, mental, and spiritual bodies. This CD combines the seven sacred vowels with bija mantras from the Vedic traditions.

"The Lost Chord" (CD)

A continuation of the sonic world created in "Chakra Chants." It features sacred mantras, overtones, and chants from the Hindu and Hebrew traditions as well as psychoacoustic frequencies and sacred ratios.

"Holy Harmony" (CD)

This CD of 72 minutes is a choral repetition of an ancient Hebraic chant combined with Healing Code Tuning Forks for deep relaxation and meditation.

"Medicine Buddha" (CD)

This album includes the Medicine Buddha mantra and the Heart of Wisdom sutra from the Tibetan Buddhist tradition invoking divine energies for healing and meditation.

These audio recordings are available from:
Spirit Music
P.O. Box 2240
Boulder, CO 80306
e-mail: info@healingsounds.com
Web site: www.healingsounds.com

"Sacred Chants" (CD)

This collection of seven chants have been selected and performed by the well-known sound healer Tom Kenyon, whose powerful and wide-ranging voice has a profound effect on a person's energy field. This collection is available from:

Tom Kenyon
P.O. Box 98
Orcas, WA 98280
Tel.: (541) 488-7870
e-mail: orders@tomkenyon.com
Web site: www.tomkenyon.com

"Healing Powers of Tone & Chant" (2 audio tapes)

This is a two-cassette audio workshop, one titled "Healing with Tone & Chant," by Don G. Campbell, and the other "Chant: Healing Power of Voice & Ear," presented by Tim Wilson. The former is an exploration of the benefits of toning and chanting and the latter is an in-depth introduction to the research and work of Dr. A. Tomatis. This is available from:

Quest Books
The Theosophical Publishing House
P.O. Box 270
Wheaton, IL 60189–0270

"Overtone Chanting Meditations" (CD and audio tape) & "The Healing Voice, a lecture and meditation" (audio tape only)

Demonstrations of overtone chanting by the internationally known workshop leader Jill Purce. These recordings are available from:

Healing Voice
20 Willow Road
London NW3 1TJ
UK
Tel.: 44 20 7435 2467
e-mail: Info@healingvoice.com
Web site: www.healingvoice.com

Overtoning Demonstration Recording (CD)

An audio recording of part of the book by Rollin Rachele (see recommended reading). For more information, contact:

Rollin Rachele, Director
Abundant Sun Ltd.

BCM Rachele
London W1N 3XX
UK
e-mail: rollin@abundantsun.com

"Gongs of the Solar System" (CD)

Based on Hans Cousto's discovery of the orbital frequencies of the planets, each planetary gong is equated with certain chakras and the enveloping sounds activate many different positive attributes of a person. Performed by gongmaster Don Conreaux. Available from:

Mysterious Tremendum
Box 318 Village Station
New York, NY 10014–0318
e-mail: gongman@escape.com
Web site: www.holistic-resonance.com

"The Singing Bowls of Tibet" (audio tape)

An in-depth lecture and demonstration on Tibetan singing bowls by the performer and acknowledged authority on the subject Frank Perry. To purchase this recording, contact:

Mountain Bell Music
Frank Perry
3 Drake Close
Ringwood
Hants BH24 1UG
UK
e-mail: Frank@frankperry.co.uk
Web site: www.frankperry.co.uk

"Six Healing Sounds" (audio tape)

This tape serves as a companion to the section "Toning the Organs of the Body" in chapter 11. It is available from:

The Healing Tao Center
P.O. Box 1194
Huntington, NY 11743
Tel.: (800) 497-1017 *or* (717) 325-9380 (overseas)
Fax: (717) 325-9357

"The Sound of Silence" & "Chanting the Chakras" (audio tapes)

These cassette tapes are produced by a prominent teacher of sacred sound chanting, Muz Murray. "The Sound of Silence" contains knowledge about the mystical and practical aspects of mantra, pranayama, and the Sanskrit alphabet as well as well-known Eastern chants. "Chanting the Chakras" has a selection of mantras for healers, including the Tantric seed sounds of the chakras. Go to the Mantra-Yoga Web site for more information:

e-mail: iqd@mantra-yoga.com
Web site: www.mantra-yoga.com

"Sounds of the Chakras" (audio tape)

An explanation and demonstration of the intonation of sounds as they relate to the chakra centers by the Tantric scholar, artist, and composer, Harish Johari.

"Primordial Tones 1" (2 CDs)

A realization in sound on two CDs by the author Joachim-Ernst Berendt (see recommended reading) of the calculations of the frequencies for the sun, moon, and earth as well as the Shiva-Shakti sound. These calculations were first put forward by Hans Cousto in his book *The Cosmic Octave*. The objective is to place listeners in sympathetic resonance with the primordial energies of these bodies and thus lead them into a meditative state.

These recordings are available from:

Destiny Recordings
Inner Traditions International
One Park Street
Rochester, VT 05767
Web site: www.InnerTraditions.com

"Life Tuning with Prima Sounds: The Discovery of Chakra Music" & "Prima Sounds" (CDs)

Prima Sounds are a series of five tones tuned to the human energy system, more specifically to the chakra centers. They are unique and not related to any other tuning system. Calculated by an Austrian professor, Dr. Arnold Keyserling, who subsequently wrote a book about his discovery and invented a musical instrument that uses these frequencies, the tuning of the tones is related to the Alpha brain waves. Through the effect of resonance between the waves of Prima Sounds and the energies of our electromagnetic field, the tones have the potential to reduce stress, increase concentration and energy, and serve as a path to open up higher consciousness. The object is for the sounds to impact the whole body. The tones are presented on two recordings, both as individual frequencies and in the form of musical compositions created by Ralph Losey. See the following Web site for ordering information: www.sun-angel.com

Recommended Reading

Practical Voice Work & Theory

Andrews, Ted. *Sacred Sounds: Transformation Through Music & Word.* St. Paul, Minn.: Llewellyn Publications, 1992.

Beaulieu, John. *Music and Sound in the Healing Arts.* Barrytown, N.Y.: Station Hill Press, 1987.

Campbell, Don. *The Roar of Silence, Healing Powers of Breath, Tone & Music.* London: The Theosophical Publishing House, 1989.

DeMohan, Elias. *The Harmonics of Sound, Color & Vibration.* Marina del Rey, Calif.: De Vorss & Co., 1994.

Dewhurst-Maddock, Olivea. *Healing With Sound: Self-help Techniques using Music and Your Voice.* London: Gaia Books Limited, 1997.

Gardner-Gordon, Joy. *The Healing Voice: Traditional & Contemporary Toning, Chanting & Singing.* Freedom, Calif.: The Crossing Press, 1993.

Gardner, Kay. *Sounding the Inner Landscape: Music As Medicine.* Shaftesbury, Dorset, UK: Element Books, 1997.

Garfield, Laeh Maggie. *Sound Medicine: Healing with Voice, Music & Song.* Berkeley, Calif.: Celestial Arts, 1987.

Gass, Robert. *Chanting: Discovering Spirit in Sound.* New York: Broadway Books, 1999.

Gaynor, Dr. Mitchell L.. *The Healing Power of Sound: Recovery from Life-Threatening Illness Using Sound, Voice, and Music*. Boston: Shambhala Publications Inc., 1999.

Goldman, Jonathan. *Healing Sounds: The Power of Harmonics*. Rochester, Vt.: Inner Traditions, 2002.

Goldman, Jonathan. *Shifting Frequencies*. Sedona, Ariz.: Light Technology Publishing, 1998.

Hale, Susan Elizabeth. *Song and Silence: Voicing The Soul*. Albuquerque, N. Mex.: La Alameda Press, 1995.

Keyes, Laurel Elizabeth. *Toning: The Creative Power of the Voice*. Marina del Rey, Calif.: De Vorss & Co., 1973.

McClellan, Randall. *The Healing Forces of Music: History, Theory and Practice*. Warwick, N.Y.: Amity House, Inc., 1988.

Newham, Paul. *The Healing Voice: How to Use the Power of Your Voice to Bring Harmony into Your Life*. Shaftesbury, Dorset, UK: Element Books, 1999.

Rachele, Rollin. *Overtone Singing Study Guide*. Amsterdam, Netherlands: Cryptic Voice Productions, 1996.

The Nature and Power of Sound

Berendt, Joachim-Ernst. *The Third Ear: On Listening to the World*. Shaftesbury, Dorset, UK: Element Books, 1988.

Berendt, Joachim-Ernst. *The World Is Sound: Nada Brahma*. Rochester, Vt.: Destiny Books, 1991.

Blofield, John. *Mantras: Secret Words of Power*. New York: Dutton Books, 1977.

Campbell, Don, ed. *Music: Physician for Times to Come*. London: Quest Books, 1991.

Campbell, Don, ed. *Music and Miracles*. London: Quest Books, 1992.

Cousto, Hans. *The Cosmic Octave: Origin of Harmony.* Mendocino, Calif.: LifeRhythm Books, 1988.

D'Angelo, James. "Resonances of the Cosmos." *Caduceus* 23 (1994).

D'Angelo, James. "The Tuning of the Universe." *The Bridge* (a journal of the Study Society), no. 7 (Summer 1991).

Edwards, Sharry. "Sound Techniques for Tuning your Health." *Nexus*, April–May 1997.

Hamel, Peter Michael. *Through Music to the Self.* Boulder, Colo.: Shambhala Publications, 1979.

Heleus, Michael. "Reconnecting with the Cosmic Bearings of Life through the Right Use of Sound." *Whole Network Journal*, Summer 1988.

Hero, Barbara. "Healing with Sound." *Caduceus* 23 (1994).

Hero, Barbara. *Lambdoma Unveiled.* 2nd ed. North Berwick, Me.: Strawberry Hill Farm Studios Press, 1992.

Jenny, Hans. *Cymatics, Volumes I & II.* Basel, Switzerland: Basilius Presse AG, 1974.

Khan, Hazrat Inayat. *The Music Of Life.* New Lebanon, N.Y.: Omega Publications, 1983.

Lalita. *Choose Your Own Mantra.* New York: Bantam Books, 1978.

Leeds, Joshua. *The Power of Sound.* Rochester, Vt.: Healing Arts Press, 2001.

Maman, Fabien. *The Role of Music in the Twenty-First Century* (Book I), *Raising Human Frequencies: The Way of Chi and the Subtle Bodies* (Book II), *Sound and Acupuncture* (Book III), and *Healing with Sound, Color, and Movement* (Book IV). Redondo Beach, Calif.: Tama-Do Press, 1997.

Manners, Dr. Peter Guy. "Cymatic and Bio-Energetic Medicine." Paper issued by the Bretforton Scientific and Medical Trust, Worcester, UK, 1988.

McIntosh, Solveig. *Hidden Faces of Ancient Indian Song.* Hampshire, UK: Ashgate Publishing Ltd., 2005.

Oldfield, Harry. "Electro-Crystal Therapy." *Kindred Spirit* 33 (Winter 1995/1996).

Rael, Joseph. *Being and Vibration.* Tulsa, Okla.: Council Oak Books, 1993.

Rouget, Gilbert. *Music and Trance.* Chicago: University of Chicago Press, 1985.

Schroeder-Sheker, Therese. "Music for the Dying." *Caduceus* 23 (1994).

Soule, Dr. Duncan. "The Sound of Inner Resonance." *Open Ear,* Fall 1994.

Steiner, Rudolf. *The Inner Nature of Music and the Experience of Tone.* London: Rudolf Steiner Press and Hudson, N.Y.: Anthroposophic Press, 1983.

Stewart, R. J. *The Spiritual Dimensions of Music.* Rochester, Vt.: Destiny Books, 1990.

Tame, David. *The Secret Power of Music.* Rochester, Vt.: Destiny Books, 1984.

Whone, Herbert. *The Hidden Face of Music.* New York: The Garden Studio, 1978.

Music Theory and Acoustics

Danielou, Alain. *Music and the Power of Sound.* Rochester, Vt.: Inner Traditions, 1995.

Godwin, Joscelyn. *Harmonies of Heaven and Earth.* Rochester, Vt.: Inner Traditions, 1987.

Godwin, Joscelyn. *Music, Mysticism, and Magic.* New York & London: Arkana Paperbacks, 1987.

Levarie, Siegmund, and Ernst Levy. *Tone: A Study in Musical Acoustics.* Kent, Ohio: Kent State University Press, 1968.

Rudhyar, Dane. *The Magic of Tone and the Art of Music.* London: Shambhala Publications, 1982.

General Interest

Alper, Frank. *Exploring Atlantis* (Vols. I, II, III). Phoenix, Ariz.: Arizona Metaphysical Society, 1986.

Baginski, Bodo, and Shalila Sharamon. *Reiki: Universal Life Energy.* Mendocino, Calif.: LifeRhythm Publications, 1988.

Bentov, Itzhak. *Stalking the Wild Pendulum: On the Mechanics of Consciousness.* Rochester, Vt.: Destiny Books, 1988.

Brennan, Barbara. *Hands of Light: A Guide Through the Human Energy Field.* New York: Bantam Books, 1988.

Bunnell, Toni. "A Tentative Mechanism for Healing." *Positive Health,* November/December 1997.

Elkington, David. *In The Name of the Gods.* Sherborne, Dorset, UK: Green Man Press, 2001.

Feuerstein, George. *Encyclopedic Dictionary of Yoga.* London: Unwin Hyman, 1990.

Freeman, Laurence, OSB. *Christian Meditation: Your Daily Practice.* Rydalmere, NSW, Australia: Hunt & Thorpe, 1994.

Gimbel, Theo. *Form, Sound, Color and Healing.* Saffron Walden, Essex, UK: The C.W. Daniel Company, 1987.

Gerber, Dr. Richard. *Vibrational Medicine* (3rd edition). Rochester, Vt.: Bear & Company, 2001.

Godwin, Joscelyn. *The Mystery of the Seven Vowels.* Grand Rapids, Mich.: Phanes Press, 1991.

Hindemith, Paul. *A Composer's World: Horizons and Limitations.* New York: Doubleday & Co., 1961.

Hislop, Dr. John S. *Conversations with Bhagavan Sri Sathya Sai Baba.* Anantapur, Andhra Pradesh, India: Sri Sathya Sai Books & Publication Trust, 1978.

Johari, Harish. *Chakras: Energy Centers of Transformation.* Rochester, Vt.: Destiny Books, 2000.

Leadbeater, C.W. *The Chakras.* London: Quest Books, 1977.

Main, John, OSB. *Moment of Christ: The Path of Meditation.* London: Darton, Longman, and Todd, 1984.

Mallasz, Gitta (transcriber). *Talking With Angels.* English translation by Robert Hinshaw. Einsiedeln, Switzerland: Daimon Verlag, 1988.

Men, Hunbatz. *Secrets of Mayan Science/Religion.* Rochester, Vt.: Bear & Company Publishing, 1990.

Metzger, Wolfgang, and Perfang Zhon. *T'ai Chi Ch'uan & Qigong: Technique and Training.* New York: Sterling Publishing Co., 1996.

Ouspensky, P. D. *In Search of the Miraculous: Fragments of an Unknown Teaching.* New York & London: Harcourt Brace and Jovanovich, 1977.

Piersall, Paul. *The Heart's Code.* London: Thorsons, 1998.

Pond, Dale. *The Physics of Love: The Ultimate Universal Laws.* Santa Fe, N.Mex.: The Message Company, 1996.

Prem, Sri Krishna. *The Yoga of the Bhagavat Gita.* Baltimore, Md.: Penguin Books, 1973.

Rendel, Peter. *Introduction to the Chakras.* Northants, UK: The Aquarian Press, 1979.

Tansley, David V. *Radionics & the Subtle Anatomy of Man.* Devon, UK: Health Science Press, 1976.

Tomatis, Dr. Alfred. *The Conscious Ear: My Life of Transformation Through Listening.* Barrytown, N.Y.: Station Hill Press, 1990.

Twitchell, Paul. *The Tiger's Fang.* Crystal, Minn.: Illuminated Way Publishing, 1988.

Watson, Lyall. *Supernature.* Garden City, N.Y.: Anchor Books, 1973.

White, Ruth. *Working With Your Chakras.* London: Judy Piatkus, 1993.

Whone, Herbert. "Music, the Way of Return." *Parabola* 5, no. 2 (Summer 1980).

Whone, Herbert. "The Power of Language." *Caduceus* 23 (1994).

ADDENDUM

The author can be contacted regarding his therapeutic sound and movement workshops at:

e-mail: healingvibes@soundspirit.co.uk
Web site: www.soundspirit.co.uk

Index

THE HEALING POWER OF THE HUMAN VOICE
CD DIRECTORY

Total recording length 72:08